CW00537657

TORQU
COMMEMORATIVES
AND
ADVERTISING
WARES

by
Virginia Brisco

TPCS

Published by
The Torquay Pottery Collectors' Society, Torre Abbey, Torquay, Devon, England

First published in 1991 by
The Torquay Pottery Collectors' Society

Text and Editorial: Virginia Brisco
Photography: Mike Mackenzie (unless otherwise stated)
Design and Production: Keith Poole

COVER PHOTOGRAPHS

Front Cover: *Three Aller Vale Coronation commemoratives. Left to right: loving cup inscribed 'Crowned June 1902'; loving cup, dark green ground, inscribed 'Crowned August 1902'; mug inscribed 'Crowned June 1911'*

Inside Front Cover: *Terracotta group known as 'You dirty boy', twenty six inches (66 cms.) tall, modelled by Giovanni Focardi. This was made by the Watcombe Pottery to advertise Pears Soap, although other examples were made by the Torquay Terracotta Company.*

Inside Back Cover: *Longpark vase, fourteen and a half inches (37 cms.) tall, made to commemorate the Coronation of King Edward VIII in 1937. Inscribed on the base 'Made at Longpark, Torquay, October 24th 1936, Frederick H. Blackler, Managing Director'. One of the pair shown in the 'Torquay Herald and Express' of 12th December 1936 (see fig. 24).*

Back Cover: *Plate, ten and a half inches (26.5 cms.) in diameter made by Watcombe to advertise both the Potteries and Spooners department store in Plymouth.*

Copyright: © 1991 TPCS

ISBN 0 9515089 1 1

Typeset, printed and bound
in Great Britain by
Redwood Press Limited
Melksham, Wiltshire

PREFACE

Commemoratives have been a popular area of collecting for many years, yet most of the books on the subject either ignore the Torquay potteries altogether or show a token item attributed to a 'small country pottery'. Clearly there is a need for information on these South Devon potteries and this book aims to fill that need by providing a comprehensive guide to the commemoratives that were made together with some of the social history behind those events. The Torquay potteries were prolific and produced commemoratives for all the coronations and jubilees between 1887 and 1953, as well as a wide variety of military, political, local and personal commemoratives – the range is vast even though the runs may sometimes be short.

The majority of Torquay commemoratives were made from local clays and decorated with traditional coloured slips and sgraffito inscriptions. The same materials and skills were used to make the famous Torquay mottowares which became the bread and butter lines of the potteries for over fifty years and which are so popular with collectors today. The success of mottowares in the early twentieth century enabled the potteries to develop a sideline in the growing market of advertising wares; advertising relies on slogans, or mottoes, which can easily be transcribed to fairly basic lines of pottery. This is a relatively new area of collecting and the book shows the great diversity of items that are available, from adaptations of traditional mottowares to promotional gimmicks.

The author has researched the subject in depth but would welcome information about pots not shown or mentioned in the book – new items are constantly coming to light, even as the book was being produced.

If you enjoy collecting Torquay pottery we hope you will join the T.P.C.S. and share your hobby with like minded enthusiasts.

ACKNOWLEDGEMENTS

Many people and organisations have helped with the production of this book, and without them the book would not have been possible. I should like to thank the following who loaned their pots for the photographs: Mr & Mrs Brian Allen, Mr Peter Applewhite, Mr & Mrs Derek Barber, Mr John Barrett, Miss Audrey Blackler, Mr & Mrs John Bowden, Miss Margaret Broderick, Mr & Mrs Derek Byram, Mr Alec Carpenter, Mr & Mrs Dennis Cockell, Mr Norman Cole, Mrs Daphne Collis, the late Mr James Cook, Mr Harold Diamond, Mrs Shirley Everett, Mr & Mrs Tom Fisher, Mr Ken Hall, Mr & Mrs Bob Hawes, Mrs Angela Hawkins, Mr Tom Jones, Mrs Olive King, Mrs Margaret Leacock, Mr & Mrs Brian Lean, Mr Melvyn Lingel, Mr William Loram, Mr & Mrs Ian Merckel, Miss Vera Payton, Mr & Mrs Keith Poole, Mr Sydney Reed, Mr & Mrs Peter Robinson, Mr Cyril Rogers, Mr & Mrs Den Rowley, Mr Michael Rowse, Mr & Mrs John Ryecraft, Mrs Joan Saunders, Mrs Jean Siney, Mr & Mrs Graham Steele, Mrs Joyce Stonelake, Mrs Jacqui Thompson, Mrs Laura Walsh, Mr & Mrs Gordon Webster, Mrs Susan Weeks, Mrs Edna White, Mr Peter Whight, Mr Paul Wilson, Mr & Mrs Ron Wood.

Photographs were taken by Mike Mackenzie with the exception of figs. 1, 8, 9, 22, 23 & 50 by Brian Everett; inside back cover by Chris Bryan; figs. 38, 43, 56, 57, 60 and 67 by the author, fig. 12 Mr & Mrs John Bowden. The photograph used for fig. 73 was given to the TPCS by the late Mrs Elsie Medland (nee Franks).

Many members of the TPCS have supplied me with background information about various commemoratives and advertising wares and I should like to thank: Mrs Barbara Baggs, Mrs Diane Blowers, Mrs Barbara Bradley, Miss Margaret Broderick, Mrs Betty Duly, Mr Alec Carpenter, Mr John Dyer, Mrs Shirley Everett, Mrs Margaret Smale.

Various individuals, organisations and companies have been most helpful, especially the following: Mr Ian Barrett, Secretary of the National Association of Master Bakers, Confectioners and Caterers; Mr F. M. Broadbent, Registrar for the Diocese of Salisbury; Mrs Brenda Cole; Mrs Angela Doughty, Exeter Cathedral Archivist; Mr Kenneth Harvey of the Radio Society of Great Britain; Mr Leslie Hough, Secretary of St Austell Old Cornwall Society; Mr Brian May of the Berthon Boat Co. Ltd.; Mr Leslie Lowndes-Pateman,

Secretary of Babbacombe and St Marychurch Traders and Hoteliers Association; Mr J. W. George Patton of the Grand Orange Lodge of Ireland; A. & F. Pears Ltd. Library & Archives Dept.; Mr J. D. Skinner of the National Federation of Sub-Postmasters; Staff at the following libraries: Barnet, Devon County (Exeter), Exmouth, Folkestone, North Yorkshire, Nottingham, Weymouth.

In addition, the help received from the following people deserves special mention: The Reverend John Copping, Vicar of St John the Baptist, Cookham Dean for researching the parish magazines and school registers; Mrs Valerie Edgecombe for information about the Torbay & Newton Vespa Club; Mr George Holden for information about the Sun of Canada Cricket Tours; the Reverend Canon A. T. Johnson, Rector of Semley, for research into St Catherine's, Sedgehill; Mr William Loram for researching the Priory Farm Dairy, Taunton and the New Zealand Rugby tours; Mr Cyril Wilson for information about pottery techniques and permission to use the photograph of his late father, Reg Wilson, in fig. 21.

Finally my thanks go to the TPCS Book Team whose hard work has enabled the book to be produced; Keith Poole, for the Design and Layout; Shirley Everett, for typing the manuscript onto computer disc; my husband Bill for much encouragement and most of the work in assembling the pots for photography and Ron Wood for financial supervision. With such a large undertaking it is possible I have omitted to thank others who contributed and I do so now.

Introduction

Commemorative wares are those pieces made to celebrate a special event such as a coronation, a marriage or a christening. Other commemoratives record more sombre occasions such as the death of a monarch, or the last firing of a pottery kiln. The history of English commemoratives goes back hundreds of years, perhaps even as far back as the Roman Empire as pieces from this era have been found with inscriptions which may relate to particular events. After the Roman occupation ended the craft of potting went into a decline from which it did not emerge until the seventeenth century with the imaginative decoration applied to slipwares and Delft style pottery.

The earliest Royal commemoratives date from this period and examples include a London Delft charger to commemorate the accession of Charles II in 1660, or a slipware dish by Thomas Toft showing the Royal Arms of England with the initials 'CR' for Charles II. Chargers were also made for marriages, and small pottery cradles to celebrate the birth of a child. These were 'show pieces' of the potters and many were inscribed with the name of the potter as part of the decoration; those could be called early advertising pieces since presumably the object of signing the piece was to encourage future orders!

During the seventeenth and eighteenth centuries commissioning commemoratives remained the prerogative of the well to do, but the Industrial Revolution brought opportunities for a much wider market. The Staffordshire potteries could manufacture china much more cheaply and transfer decorations opened up the possibilities for mass produced commemoratives. Improvements in transport and communications made people more aware of what was happening in the outside world and the increasing affluence of the lower middle classes meant more people had money to spend on 'consumer goods'. Commemoratives for Royal events began to increase in popularity during the first half of the nineteenth century; however Prince Albert's death in 1861 sent Queen Victoria into virtual seclusion which made the monarchy seem remote, and perhaps even irrelevant. The Jubilee in 1887 was to change all that! Queen Victoria's estrangement from her people was reconciled and the British public could glory in patriotism and the Empire. Royalist sentiments have remained popular ever since.

The vast majority of Victorian, and later, commemoratives were mass produced slipcast wares with transfer printing. However, alongside this were the smaller runs by local potteries which continued the older tradition of slip and s'graffito work, or majolica styles. One area which was prolific during the late nineteenth and twentieth centuries was South Devon, centred around Torquay.

Devon had a long history of potting, mainly in the North, due to abundant supplies of local clay. However in the late 1860's new deposits of clay were discovered at Watcombe, just outside Torquay, and this spawned a whole new industry of potting which lasted until the 1960's; during this time some twenty or more potteries were making what became known generically as 'Torquay Pottery' even though some of the potter-

1

ies were as far away as Exeter, Bovey Tracey and Plymouth!

At first the Watcombe Terracotta Clay Company and its rival, the Torquay Terracotta Company, concentrated on fine terracotta wares and many of their earliest commemoratives are in this style. However, during the 1880's and 1890's they began to concentrate more on glazed art pottery because terracotta was going out of fashion – it was perhaps too plain for most flamboyant Victorian taste! In 1881 a new art pottery was opened at Aller Vale, just outside Newton Abbot, to produce slip and s'graffito wares using local materials according to the principles of the Arts & Crafts Movement. With the increasing popularity of these wares the Watcombe Pottery adopted similar styles, as did many new potteries which sprang up during the early twentieth century. The vast majority of Torquay commemoratives and advertising wares are decorated in slip and s'graffito although collectors should look out for the rarer examples of the terracotta, art pottery and faience style pieces.

FROM *THE POTTERY GAZETTE*

May 1st 1917.

'The Royal Aller Vale and Watcombe Art Potteries of Newton Abbot, Devon, can fairly claim to have established a native English potting industry which owes nothing to foreign influences. On them has fallen the mantle of the makers of the homely wares, richly coloured and vigorously executed, through which the 'Art of the English Potter' won the admiration of many discerning connoisseurs, including even M. Solon, artist and Frenchman, and pre-eminent master of the theory and practice of pottery decoration'.

SOUTH DEVON POTTERIES

Watcombe Pottery, St. Marychurch, 1869–1962.

Torquay Terracotta Company, Hele Cross, Torquay, 1875–c.1905, reopened as Royal Torquay Pottery Co. to c.1939.

Aller Vale Pottery, Kingskerswell, 1881–c.1924.

Longpark Pottery Co., Newton Road, Torquay, began 1883 as a terracotta company c.1903–1957 Art Pottery and Mottowares.

Exeter Art Pottery, Exeter, 1891–1896, then known as Hart and Moist to 1935.

Tor Vale Pottery, Teignmouth Road, Torquay, c.1913/14; then taken over by Lemon and Crute 1926; became Daison Art Pottery to c.1932.

Barton Pottery, Torquay, c.1921–39.

Devon Tors Pottery, Bovey Tracey, 1921–Devonmoor, c.1922–1977.

Plymouth Pottery, Plymouth, c.1926–? (short lived).

Bovey Tracey Art Pottery — subsidiary of Royal Torquay in 1930s.

Dartmouth Pottery, 1948–Sandygate, 1950.

Babbacombe Pottery, 1952–St. Marychurch Pottery, 1962–69.

ROYAL COMMEMORATIVES

During the 1870's the output of the Watcombe and Torquay Terracotta companies consisted mainly of unglazed terracotta urns, vases, statuettes and busts in classical styles. However, as early as 1872 the Watcombe Pottery commissioned its first Royal commemorative, a terracotta bust of H.R.H. Princess Louise, Queen Victoria's sixth child (fig. 1). This bust is 13 inches (33 cms.) tall and was 'modelled expressly for the Company by Leifchild' and published in March 1872. A companion piece was modelled of H.R.H. Princess Louise's husband, the Marquis of Lorne, but since these are much rarer, this would suggest that they could be purchased separately. The couple had married a year earlier, on 21st March 1871 at St. George's Chapel, Windsor. H.R.H. Princess Louise was a sculptor herself and took a great interest in the potteries of Britain, making several visits to Torquay. In 1895, whilst on a visit to the Aller Vale Pottery she delighted the workers by sitting at their bench and sketching her ideas for decoration. She suggested they should use local features, such as a blue butterfly found in the South Hams area; this idea was adopted and the new line called 'Princess Louise Ware'!

As the fashion for classical styles declined in the 1880's the potteries widened their ranges to include busts of contemporary figures. Most of these were of politicians, church leaders or military figures, but some Royal figures were included, such as a pair of 4 inch busts of T.R.H. Prince and Princess of Wales. These busts were made by the Torquay Terracotta Company, possibly to celebrate the Prince and Princess's Silver Wedding in 1888, but are rarely found.

Fig. 1. Pair of terracotta busts thirteen inches (33cm.)tall of Princess Louise and the Marquis of Lorne. Modelled for the Watcombe Pottery by Leifchild 1872.

FROM *THE ART JOURNAL* 1872

'Other remarkable works are statuettes of the Princess Louise, the Marquis of Lorne, the late Charles Dickens etc. of which great numbers have been sold; . . .'

The Golden Jubilee of 1887

1887 marked the fiftieth anniversary of H.M. Queen Victoria's accession to the throne; Jubilee Day was 21st June and was celebrated with church services, parades, ox roasts or tea parties and, of course, the acquisition of commemoratives. The Watcombe Pottery published a bust of Queen Victoria from an original by W. C. Lawton who was employed there in the 1880's. Lawton spent most of his working life in the Staffordshire Potteries but had gone to Devon in the 1880's for about six years chiefly on health grounds. He was responsible

THE POTTERY GAZETTE

Obituary in September 1st 1933 for Mr William Charles Lawton the well known pottery modeller.
'He was a native of Hanley and practically the whole of his working life had been spent in the Potteries, where he executed a good deal of sterling work largely on his own account as a modeller to the trade . . . There was an interregnum of about six years when Mr.Lawton, chiefly on health grounds, worked at his profession in Devonshire at the Royal Aller Vale and Watcombe Art Potteries'.

Fig. 2. Detail of the lid of a Watcombe 1887 commemorative jug, to show the halfcrown coin set in a silver rim. The obverse shows Queen Victoria with a 'bun' hairstyle and it is dated 1887.

for modelling many of Watcombe's finest busts including General Gordon, Lord Salisbury and John Bright. Lawton's bust of Queen Victoria is 13 inches tall and is very delicately modelled (fig. 7) Presumably the Pottery were well pleased with it because they adapted the design to make a smaller bust 6 inches tall, which they issued for the Diamond Jubilee in 1897 – the later model though, lacks much of the vitality of its predecessor!

Another terracotta commemorative issued by the Watcombe Pottery for the 1887 Jubilee was a jug with a deeply ribbed and bulbous body rather like a coil pot that has not been smoothed out. Underneath the spout is a cameo of the head of the Queen surrounded by a laurel wreath. The jugs were sold in three variations – the plainest being all terracotta, the middle version having a narrow silver rim and the most elaborate form is shown in fig 7. This has a silver rim and spout, and a silver cover; inset in the cover is a half-crown coin dated 1887 showing the young Queen with a bun hairstyle. Indeed, without the

coin and hallmark it might be difficult for collectors to date the jug because the same cameo was used for the 1897 commemoratives. This was possible because the heads were applied by a process known as sprigging; the head and laurel wreath surround were moulded separately and then applied to the jug. Sometimes sprigs were traded between the potteries. Sprigged ornamentation is much finer than if it had been moulded as part of the pot. Silver work on the Watcombe 1887 jug was executed for Leuchars of London and Paris.

Fig. 3. Detail of the sprigged head of Queen Victoria which was used on the 1887 and 1897 Watcombe commemoratives and the Aller Vale 1901 'In Memoriam' loving cups.

Early Aller Vale commemoratives

Early Aller Vale commemoratives were made by adapting their standard patterns of decoration, usually simply by adding a suitable inscription. One such example is a vase decorated in slips with white roses on a blue ground and with a s'graffito inscription 'The Rose of York 6th July 1893' (fig. 6). This was made to commemorate the marriage of H.R.H. Princess Mary (May) of Teck to H.R.H. the Duke of York. The decoration is done in a style which the Pottery termed 'barbotine' and these formed the major output of the Pottery in the 1880's and 1890's. Early barbotine pieces are on a thick slip ground, usually blue, although sometimes brown/beige, which has an orange peel texture. Many different flower decorations were used although roses were always popular and especially suitable for the White Rose of York!

Aller Vale also made another vase decorated with a white rose which must be a Royal commemorative because it is surrounded by National emblems such as shamrocks and oak leaves (fig. 6). This vase is also decorated in slips although more thinly applied than on barbotine pieces. This style of decoration was becoming popular in the 1890's and was later given the pattern code K2 which can often be seen incised on the base. Barbotine vases often show signs of wear because the thickly applied slips are prone to 'scuff' when in use so more thinly applied colours were used. On stylistic grounds it would seem very likely that this is also a commemorative for the marriage of the Duke of York.

A year after their marriage, the Duke and Duchess of York produced their first son, H.R.H. Prince Edward, who briefly became H.M. Edward VIII, before his abdication in 1936. This event was commemorated by the Aller Vale Pottery in the form of two handled loving cups and beakers (fig. 6). The decoration is based on their standard line, known as Q1, which consisted of yellow, blue and red pigments on a cream ground done in majolica style. This commemorative has been embellished with the addition of a rose around which is the s'graffito inscription 'Prince Edward of York'; below this is the motto 'Bright be the stars on the eve of St. John, Luckie the babe that is born thereon'. The Prince was born on 23rd June 1894, the day before the feast of St. John the Baptist. Very few commemoratives were made for the birth of Prince Edward and consequently they are highly sought by collectors.

The Diamond Jubilee of 1897

The Aller Vale Pottery do not appear to have made any 1887 commemoratives, but they certainly made up for it in 1897 with the Diamond Jubilee. Several versions were made based on the Q1 and Kerswell Daisy patterns as well as some completely new styles (fig. 4). One of these was a plain brown jug with a pinched spout, which has a cameo head of Victoria under the spout. The head is framed with national flowers – roses, thistles and shamrocks, and is surrounded by a piped inscription done in slip 'We therefore have great cause of thankfulness'. Two versions of this jug have been seen, on one the flowers are picked out in colours and on the other the jug has simply been dipped in a honey glaze which gives it a warm glow. The same brown jugs were also made with just a simple cream slip inscription 'Diamond Jubilee 1897' but these look rather sombre for such a joyous occasion.

Although the practice of giving

Fig. 4. Selection of Aller Vale commemoratives for the Diamond Jubilee in 1897. The large jug at the back is seven inches (18 cms.) tall and is decorated in the Q1 pattern. The jug at the bottom left has a white sprigged head of Victoria with heraldic plants forming a frame picked out in natural colours; on the right, a similar jug has been dipped in an amber glaze.

local commemoratives began early in the nineteenth century it did not became widespread until the Coronation in 1902. Only one example from the Torquay Potteries has been seen earlier than 1902 and that is an Aller Vale two handled loving cup decorated with the Kerswell Daisy pattern and inscribed 'Horton, Bucks.' and 'VR 1837–1897' (fig. 12). The Leighton Buzzard Observer of Tuesday June 29th 1897 carried a report of the Jubilee celebrations at Horton which were fairly typical of villages all over the country. All the village men were entertained to lunch at Horton House and were provided with 'the usual English fare of roast and boiled beef, hams and plum pudding . . . to which

full justice was done'. Then 'at half past three the men, women and children partook of tea, and at half past nine supper was provided'. During the afternoon and evening there were games, running and jumping and a cricket match – although one wonders how any of the men played cricket after such a heavy lunch in mid-Summer! The Leighton Buzzard Observer noted 'A pleasant feature was the presentation by Miss Mary Buckmaster to each woman and child of a Jubilee present in the shape of teapots, cups and saucers, beakers, etc. which gave very great pleasure to the recipients'. It would seem likely that the Aller Vale loving cups were part of this presentation yet so far *only* loving cups have been seen – perhaps the teapots, cups and saucers, etc. were commissioned from another pottery!

The Watcombe Pottery also produced commemoratives for the Diamond Jubilee although they are much rarer than the Aller Vale examples. During the late 1890's the Watcombe Pottery experienced financial problems which probably explains why they adapted existing lines for their commemoratives. Fig. 7 shows a jug and two beakers decorated with prunus blossom on a green ground and with the same sprigged head as had been used in 1887. Only the jug is inscribed with the dates which suggests that these were sold as water or lemonade sets rather than individually. The blossom decoration was very popular at Watcombe and was used for over twenty years on items as varied as egg cups, teasets, salad bowls and tobacco jars.

Death of H.M. Queen Victoria 1901

When Queen Victoria died in 1901 surprisingly few 'in memoriam' pieces were made, probably because public saturation had been reached with the Diamond Jubilee and the Boer War. Aller Vale made a few tygs and mugs with the head of the Queen surrounded by laurel leaves but they are rather crudely made and lack the charm of the earlier pieces – perhaps because they were made in haste! These commemoratives have Victoria's date of birth and death together with a simple inscription such as 'In her was Mother, Wife and Queen' (from Tennyson's poem 'To the Queen' 1851) or 'She wrought her people lasting good' which was also used on pieces for the Diamond Jubilee. The head on these pots is identical to those on the 1887 and 1897 Watcombe commemoratives which sug-

Fig. 5. 'In Memoriam' commemoratives for the death of Queen Victoria in 1901. The loving cups were made by Aller Vale, and the shoe by Hart and Moist at Exeter.

gest that the same sprigs were used. This would be highly probable because the two potteries came under common ownership in 1900. John Phillips, who started the Aller Vale Art Pottery in 1881, had died in 1896, and the following year the Works were sold to Hexter Humpherson & Co, clay merchants, of Kingsteignton. When the Watcombe Pottery went bankrupt in 1900 Hexter Humpherson bought them out too and the companies were combined as The Royal Aller Vale and Watcombe Art Potteries. Although there was an interchange of personnel and ideas the two Potteries continued to operate independently and many decorations remained exclusive to one or other of the Potteries.

A more unusual in memoriam piece is a small shoe which was made by Hart and Moist at Exeter (fig. 5). The shoe is a copy of Queen Victoria's first shoe and was reproduced by many potteries as a souvenir. However, Hart and Moist specifically advertised theirs as 'Our late beloved Queen Victoria's first shoe' and as such must be considered a commemorative of her death.

Coronation of H.M. King Edward VII 1902

Queen Victoria was succeeded by her son, Albert Edward, who became King Edward VII and soon plans were made for his Coronation on 26th June 1902. There was enormous public enthusiasm for this event – after all, few people could even remember the last Coronation – and consequently an upsurge in patriotism and Imperialist sentiment. Sometimes this nationalism bordered on the eccentric, as is evidenced by an editorial in The Devon Evening Express of 27th November 1901 which commented: 'The King, I am glad to note, has decided

HER LATE MAJESTY

QUEEN VICTORIA'S

First pair of little Shoes,

Expressly reproduced in ART POTTERY by

HART & MOIST,

The Royal Devon Art Pottery

EXETER.

(HART & MOIST supply only through special Agents, one Agent being appointed for every Town in Great Britain).

This little Shoe is a careful reproduction in Royal Devon Art Pottery of our late beloved QUEEN VICTORIA'S first Shoe, as made for her in the year 1819, as the then infant Princess Victoria:—the Bootmaker, who received the order, having made and preserved a third Shoe, which he kept as a memento and curiosity and the same has been carefully copied and reproduced in "Royal Devon Art Pottery."

that Americans are not to be admitted to the Coronation, even though they may come arrayed in gorgeous vestments and ropes of pearls and diamonds... The pageant will be paid for by the British taxpayer, and until every taxpayer who may wish to view the ceremony finds a seat, there must be no admittance for the representatives – male or female – of foreign shoddydem'.

However, as Coronation Day approached it became clear that the King was unwell; the doctors diagnosed appendicitis but the King still hoped he would be well enough for the Coronation to go ahead so the public were told it was lumbago. The appendicitis turned to peritonitis and on the 23rd June the King was told an operation must be performed at once or he would most certainly die – the Coronation had to be postponed. The British people were devastated by the news – from the capital to small villages preparations were well advanced for the celebrations. The King wished the festivities to go ahead and many complied with this command, yet in all places a cloud of gloom hung over the event; some villages abandoned the sports and parades whilst still holding the teas to avoid wasting all the food. The good news though was that the King's operation was a success and after convalescence the Coronation went ahead on 9th August. By that time most of the Indian Princes, Colonial Premiers and Royal relatives had gone home. There would have probably been room for the rich Americans after all!

The Torquay Potteries produced more commemoratives for the 1902 Coronation than for any other event (see fig. 16). Most carry the June date although the ones bearing the correct date are eagerly sought by collectors as they are much rarer. The most popular commemoratives were beakers and those made by Watcombe and Aller Vale bear a remarkable similarity. The beakers were made either of brown or white clay which was dipped in slip, sprigged busts of the King and Queen were applied, usually with a crown between them, and the heads framed with a garland of national plants such as roses, thistles and shamrocks with a suitable s'graffito inscription. The brown clay beakers were dipped in cream slip, the white (or sometimes pinky buff colour) were dipped in blue or green, so that the inscriptions were incised through the slip exposing the clay colour. The heads were in several shades from brown to buff or white. Usually the beakers were dipped in clear glaze, although occasionally a honey coloured glaze was used.

Many beakers were given to children by the Town Council, Church or local benefactor. Researching the history of these pieces can provide a fascinating hobby for the commemorative collector and may well reveal how many examples were made, and hence their rarity, although, of course, many will have undoubtedly got broken in the intervening years.

At Shaftesbury, Dorset, the children were presented with Aller Vale beakers in blue which were embellished with a round cameo seal and the inscription 'The Borough of Shaftesbury'; these were distributed to over 800 children by the Mayoress, Mrs.Imber. Shaftesbury's Coronation Celebrations took place on the original day, 26th June, and began with a service at the parish church, combining it with the unveiling of a memorial slab to a local member of the Dorset Imperial Yeomanry who had died during the Boer War – it was indeed a sombre occasion!

At Holsworthy, Devon, it was decided to abandon all the festivities planned for 26th June and to await news of the King's recovery; eventually festivities were held on the new Coronation Day, 9th August, when Mr. James Higgs J.P. presented Coronation mugs to the children. The 'Weekly News' of 21st June 1902 described these mugs: 'Holsworthy townspeople and the Hamlet inhabitants have subscribed £80 towards the festivities. Over £20 is to be expended in Coronation souvenirs in the shape of a milk horn, manufactured by the Aller Vale Pottery Company. The horn, which is of a pretty design, in addition to bearing effigies of the King and Queen will also bear the town or Stanhope coat-of-arms, by permission of Earl Stanhope, the Lord of the Manor, and a suitable inscription'.

Unfortunately the newspaper did not say how many children there were, although the total number of parishioners was about 1,000. Although the report says the beakers were made by the Aller Vale Pottery they are backstamped 'Watcombe', the confusion presumably arising because the companies were known as 'The Royal Aller Vale and Watcombe Art Potteries' whilst operating from two addresses.

The Watcombe Pottery also made commemorative beakers for children at Cookham Dean, Berkshire, but these carry the rarer date of 9th August 1902. These beakers were given by the Parish Church to all schoolchildren and the Infant School Log Book records that on September 9th 1902 'the Vicar visited to get number of children on the Register for gifts of Coronation mugs'. The Registers indicate that there were 101 children in the Infants School and 182 at the Junior School so presumably about 300 mugs would have been made. The Parish Magazine of January 1903 recorded that the Coronation mugs and carriage cost £9.15.1d. (£9.75), a remarkably low sum even in those days for such beautiful Coronation mementos. The Parish Council must have been pleased with the beakers because they went back to the Aller Vale Pottery to order similar commemoratives for the 1911 Coronation.

At Cookham Dean the Coronation beakers were given to schoolchildren only, but in some parishes, such as Sedgehill, Wiltshire all children re-

FROM *THE PARISH MAGAZINE* OF ST. JOHN THE BAPTIST

Cookham Dean, Berkshire, November 1902.

The cups given to the children, in commemoration of the Coronation of the King and Queen, were distributed on Monday, October 6th. They were specially made for us at Watcombe Pottery in Devonshire, and have been much admired. They are certainly far more artistic and worth having than most of those we have noticed in shop windows, whether in London or elsewhere. In years to come they will be a very interesting memento of an event which touched England and English-speaking people throughout the world than anything else that has happened in living memory (save perhaps the death of Queen Victoria) so that we hope the children will be encouraged to value them highly and to take every care of them'.

ceived them; one elderly resident recalled how her sister was given one and she was only 6 weeks old at the time! Two versions of the Aller Vale Sedgehill beakers have been seen both with identical cameos of a church but one being inscribed 'St. Margaret's Church, Sedgehill, Wilts.' and the other 'St. Catherine's Church, Sedgehill, Wilts'. The Salisbury Diocesan Registrar has no evidence of any church dedicated to St. Margaret in the parish of Sedgehill and the Kelly's Directories of 1898 and 1903 do

Fig. 7. Watcombe 1887 and 1897 commemoratives. The terracotta jug has a sprigged head of Victoria under the spout, and a half crown coin set in the lid, dated 1887. The large bust of Queen Victoria is thirteen inches (33 cms.) tall, excluding socle, and was modelled by W. C. Lawton for the 1887 Golden Jubilee. This design was adapted to make the small model, shown on the left, which was issued for the 1897 Diamond Jubilee. The stein jug and two beakers were most probably sold as a tap set because only the jug is dated '1837–1897'. The decoration of prunus blossom on a green ground was very popular for over twenty years.

Fig. 6. Early Aller Vale Royal commemoratives. Left and right: two handled mugs seven and a half inches (19 cms.) tall to commemorate the birth of Prince Edward of York in 1894. The decoration is a version of the Q1 pattern. Blue vase decorated with white roses done in thick slip in 'barbotine' style, inscribed under the roses 'The rose of York 6th July 1893' – to commemorate the marriage of Princess Mary of Teck to the Duke of York. The green vase is believed to commemorate the same event.

not list a St. Margarets from other denominations, so why this dedication was used remains a mystery. Sedgehill was a chapelry in the Parish of Berwick St. Leonard until 1914; it then separated from that parish and joined with a portion of East Knoyle to form the Parish of Sedgehill with St. Catherine's as the parish church. The St. Margaret's beakers are doubly curious because, in addition to being dedicated to a church that did not exist, there is no green used in the decoration, the thistles, shamrocks and leaves being painted in shades of blue. The reason for this becomes obvious when the St. Margaret's beakers are compared with their St. Catherine's counterparts. The St. Catherine's beakers have been dipped in an amber glaze and, on close examination, they too are decorated in blue which becomes green when the glaze is applied. The St. Margaret's beakers were decorated in the same way but they were dipped in a clear glaze, thus retaining the original colours.

Apart from children's souvenir beakers, the Torquay Potteries made many other versions for sale in shops, or as special commissions. The most magnificent of those is an Aller Vale

Loving Cup and stand which is eighteen and a half inches tall overall (fig. 16). The style of decoration is simlar to the beakers, but is of a much higher quality and was done by Charles Collard; the reverse of the cup and the foot are decorated with coloured scrolls done in slips. Around the side of the stand is a patriotic inscription:

Edward VII by the Grace of God
Of the United Kingdom of Great
    Britain and Ireland
And of all the Dominions beyond
    the sea
King, Defender of the Faith,
    Emperor of India
Crowned June 1902

Only one complete example of the cup and stand has been seen although there are at least two other identical stands without cups. Aller Vale also made two smaller versions of the cup with a s'graffito inscription on the reverse; the smallest cups, five inches tall, are inscribed 'Crowned June 1902' whereas the middle size, six inches tall, seem to all carry the correct date 'Crowned August 9th 1902'. Both sizes are inscribed on the reverse:

Fig. 8. Two beakers made by Watcombe for the 1902 Coronation. The one on the left was for 'Morwenstow' and the one on the right for 'Holsworthy'.

Fig. 9. Reverse of Fig. 8.

Fig. 10. Teapot, sugar bowl and milk jug made by Hart and Moist. The s'graffito inscription is
'Commemoration of King Edward VII crowned June 26th 1902'.

Send them Victorious
Happy and Glorious
Long to reign over us
God save them both.

Both Aller Vale and Watcombe made commemorative jugs and one Watcombe example is most unusual in that it only has a bust of the King which is surrounded by lilies of the valley; the inscription on the reverse is simply: 'A souvenir of the Coronation of King Edward VII 1902. Collectors should also look for the commemorative set of teapot, sugar bowl and milk jug which was made by Hart and Moist (fig. 10). The decoration on these is rather crudely done, consisting of two crossed flags of England and the inscription 'Commemoration of King Edward VII Crowned June 26th 1902' on the front and 'Long live the King' on the reverse. These pieces are rarely stamped with the pottery mark but their style makes them quite distinctive.

Sometimes collectors may come across pieces that look like Torquay Pottery but which are marked only with the name of retail outlets; this can cause confusion. Examples are Aller Vale tygs and jugs made for the 1902 Coronation which are stamped on the base 'John Ford & Co. Edinboro'. This firm was Edinburgh's principal manufacturer of flint glassware during the late nineteenth century, and they also had a shop in Princes Street from 1891 to 1926, which is presumably where the commemoratives were sold. Green jugs were made with the heads of King and Queen but with the inscription in Scottish dialect:

Send them victorious
Happy and Glorious
Lang to reign ower us
God save them baith.

13

Another version was made which was decorated with a cockerel (one of Aller Vale's standard lines) and inscribed 'Dhai gleidh an Righ' and 'God save the King'; this is undated but was almost certainly made for the 1902 Coronation. Another agent who bought from several of the Torquay Potteries was Sir Joseph Causton and Sons Ltd.,of London. Although the company were mainly printers, they commissioned special lines of match-strikers, ashtrays etc. which were advertising pieces for drinks companies. One such piece, a matchstriker for 'John Groves and Sons Ltd., Brewers, Weymouth' was also a Coronation commemorative and had the additional inscription: 'Edward VII 1902 Health to King Edward' – a very rare combination advertising and Royal commemorative.

Fig. 11. Aller Vale double handled beaker made for the 1902 Coronation. Unusual in that it is decorated with a cockerel and a Gaelic inscription 'Dhai gleidh an Righ'. The base has an impressed stamp for 'John Ford' which was an outlet in Edinburgh.

Fig. 12. Two handled mug, decorated with the Kerswell Daisy pattern, and inscribed '1837 VR 1897' with 'Horton, Bucks.' on the reverse. Made by Aller Vale.

Fig. 13. *Coronation commemoratives 1902 and 1911. The two beakers were both made for the Parish of St. John the Baptist, Cookham Dean; on the left, a Watcombe version made for the 1902 Coronation and inscribed with the correct date August 9th. On the right, the Aller Vale version made for the 1911 Coronation. Teapot and cup and saucer made by Watcombe for the 1911 Coronation; the saucer is decorated with shamrocks which is the correct match for the cup.*

Royal visits

Once King Edward and Queen Alexandra's Coronation was over the commemorative trade dropped dramatically. The Pottery Gazette lamented this, and in July 1905 they commented 'Pottery forms such an interesting and often useful, permanent record of passing events that we are really surprised that dealers do not more frequently have souvenirs in china of local happenings prepared for them'. Obviously the Pottery Trade had an interest in promoting the sale of souvenirs, and there seemed to be a growing demand for holiday mementoes as more people were able to go on excursions and holidays. The Torquay Potteries expanded rapidly to cope with the souvenir trade and their mottowares, decorated with scrolls, ships, cockerels or cottages and a witty or amusing motto, became their bread and butter lines for over fifty years. 'Local happenings' were commemorated too and occasionally these were Royal visits.

The Aller Vale Pottery produced a beaker decorated with coloured scrolls which was inscribed 'H.R.H. Duke and Duchess of York July 1899' with no indication as to which event this commemorated – these beakers are rarely seen! A more common commemorative for a Royal visit was that produced by Watcombe in 1909 for the visit of the Prince and Princess of Wales to Chewton Mendip (fig. 14). The Royal couple went on many tours, both at home and in the Colonies, and were very popular with the people. In June 1909 they toured the estates of the Duchy of Cornwall, staying with Lord Bath at Longleat House. The event was extensively reported in the 'Bath Daily Chronicle' 'by our own reporter in a motor car' – to prove that he really was in a motor car with the Royal pair's entourage, the reporter carefully recorded the speed of the car at various points and the decoration on almost every house!! June 23rd began with a drive through villages around Frome, Laverton and Midsomer Norton before stopping for Luncheon at Chewton Priory, the home of the Earl and Countess Waldegrave. After lunch the tour continued around Harptree and Farringdon Gurney before finishing at Shepton Mallet. An interesting comparison can be made between the various souvenirs given to the chil-

Fig. 14. Mug three inches (8 cms.)tall made by Watcombe and decorated with Prince of Wales feathers in s'graffito. Inscribed on the reverse: 'In commemoration of the visit of the Prince and Princess of Wales to Chewton Mendip June 23rd 1909'.

Fig. 15. Selection of items made for the Coronation in 1911. The dark coloured mugs and beaker at the back were made by Watcombe and are on a dark green ground; Harry Cole was employed at the Pottery and decorated his own mug. The teapot and cup and saucer are also by Watcombe; the saucer is a 'mis-match' as the original one would have been decorated with shamrocks. The four mugs at the front and the one on the far right were made at the Crown Dorset Pottery at Poole – they are decorated with either sprigged heads of the King and Queen or a slip trailed 'G. R.' The cream mug to the right of the teapot handle and the Cookham Dean beaker were made by Aller Vale.

16

dren to commemorate the Royal visit: at Shepton Mallet each child received a specially designed box of chocolates, at Midsomer Norton they were given a commemorative medal and a bun, but at Chewton Mendip they got a Watcombe commemorative! Whilst collectors might be grateful for the latter, one suspects the children would have preferred the chocolates or the bun!

Coronation of H.M. King George V 1911

Within a year of the Somerset tour, King Edward VII had died and the Prince and Princess of Wales became King George V and Queen Mary; the Coronation was arranged for June 22nd 1911. The Torquay Potteries again produced a wide variety of commemoratives although mostly they copied the style of the 1902 wares. In some cases they were almost repeat orders by previous customers, such as the Town Council at Shaldon, near Teignmouth, who ordered blue beakers from Aller Vale for the August 1902 Coronation and cream mugs and beakers from Watcombe in 1911.

The most frequently found Watcombe commemoratives for the 1911 Coronation are green with busts of the King and Queen in relief and icing type inscription done in white slip. On the front is usually 'Crowned June 1911' over the heads and on the reverse 'Long may they reign'. Place

> ## FROM THE COOKHAM DEAN, BERKSHIRE, PARISH MAGAZINE
>
> **July 1911**
> The Coronation Cups are being specially made for our children at the Royal Watcombe Pottery Works. St.Marychurch, Torquay. We hope to receive and to distribute them to those children whose names were on the Registers of our Schools on April 1st, or have since joined the Schools, and also to those children at the Council School, who are resident in Cookham Dean, and whose names were on the Register on the above date.
>
> *The Coronation Cups were distributed to about 180 children on 27th July 1911 by the Vicar and Mrs. Jackson. The expenditure amounted to £39.19.0d. (£39.95) but this included the tea and entertainments provided for the children on a miserably damp Coronation Fete on 23rd June, as well as the cost of the commemoratives.*

Fig. 16. Double page spread overleaf: Selection of items all commemorating the 1902 Coronation of King Edward VII and Queen Alexandra. Giant loving cup and stand eighteen and a half inches (47 cms.) overall made at the Aller Vale Pottery and decorated by Charles Collard. Top row left to right: Aller Vale two handled mug with sprigged heads of the King and Queen; Watcombe mug decorated with forget-me-not pattern and sprigged bust of the King – the motto is simply 'Tak a wee drappie' with no reference to the Coronation!; Matchstriker which also advertises 'John Groves' brewery at Weymouth; Watcombe jug with handle moulded in form of acanthus leaves and large bust of the King; Aller Vale double handled tyg decorated with a cockerel and Gaelic inscription; Hart and Moist teapot, sugar bowl and milk jug. Middle row: Watcombe beaker, inscribed on the reverse 'Parish of St. John Baptist Cookham Dean God save the King'; Watcombe beaker with sprigged busts of the King and Queen, dated 'June 1902'; Watcombe beaker with Stanhope coat of arms on the reverse and the inscription 'Town and Hamlets, Holsworthy'; Aller Vale jug with dark green ground and inscription in Scottish dialect – stamped on base 'John Ford and Co. Edinburgh'; Aller Vale beaker with cameo of a church and the inscription 'St. Catherine's Church Sedgehill Wilts' – under an amber glaze; beaker with same cameo but inscribed 'St. Margaret's Church Sedgehill Wilts' and with a clear glaze; Aller Vale beaker with sprigged heads on reverse; obverse of second Aller Vale beaker inscribed 'St. Margaret's Church Sedgehill'. Bottom row: all Aller Vale – note the way some have white and some buff clay sprigged heads. The beaker on the far right has a sprigged seal for the Borough of Shaftesbury.

names such as 'Lyndhurst' or 'Minstead' are sometimes found, but a new innovation was the addition of a personal name, such as 'Harry Cole' (who worked at the Pottery) or a message such as 'To Gordon from Dad'. Collectors should also look for the rare Watcombe commemorative teapots and matching cups and saucers – these are on a cream ground (fig. 13).

Sometimes collectors may come across small commemorative mugs which look like Torquay pottery but are invariably unmarked (fig. 17). These were made by the Crown Dorset Pottery at Poole. This Pottery was started in 1905 by Charles Collard who had previously worked in the Torquay Potteries and who decorated the giant loving cup and stand in the centre of pages 18 and 19. Most Crown Dorset wares, especially in the early years, were decorated in Torquay styles, so it is easy for the inexperienced collector to be confused. The Crown Dorset commemoratives are usually inferior in quality and design to their South Devon counterparts; two different types have been seen, one with sprigged heads of the King and Queen and the other with a slip painted 'GR' instead of heads; they were made for the Borough of Poole and the parishes of Lytchett Matravers and Sturminster Marshall, all in Dorset.

Coronation Day was wet and miserable over almost all the country and this affected the Coronation celebrations. At Poole the Council, who allocated £1,000 from the rates towards the festivities, had hired a marquee 200 ft. long to house the 800 'aged poor of the borough' for their lunch party. As the weather deteriorated even further it was decided that the children's teas would also have to take place inside the marquee – but, as

Fig. 17. Mug made by the Crown Dorset Pottery for the 1911 Coronation. Note the poor quality of the sprigged heads.

over 6,000 sodden children began to arrive total chaos reigned. The Poole 'Guardian' reported on the 'distressing scenes' at the tea party with 'juveniles helping themselves from the hampers', anxious parents looking for their children, and Boy Scouts sent out to search for the 'juveniles who had strayed in all directions'. To make matters worse, the Coronation mugs were not ready either and the 'Guardian' reported: 'Further, there was great disappointment in the matter of the Coronation mugs. Of the 7,000 ordered by the Poole Town Council, to be made of Poole clay in Poole, for presentation to the children, only about 4,000 were ready. These were distributed first to the girls and then, as far as they would go, to the boys. The remainder, when made, will be sent to the schools'. For most children in Poole, Coronation Day 1911 was a day best forgotten!

Silver Jubilee 1935

The Silver Jubilee of King George V and Queen Mary was celebrated on 6th May 1935 with as much patriotic fervour as previous Coronations. Public buildings to humble cottages were decorated with Union Jacks and there were the usual street parties, bonfires, carnivals and games, making for a really colourful occasion. By contrast, the commemoratives produced by the Watcombe Pottery decidedly lacked colour, being simply decorated in relief with heads of the King and Queen and a s'graffito inscription 'Silver Jubilee G M 1910–1935' (fig. 18). Some of these had place names on the reverse, such as 'Walton on Naze' or were personalised with inscriptions such as 'Albert Williams October 4th 1935' – perhaps commemorating a birth or a christening. Most Watcombe Jubilee commemoratives are mugs, although collectors should look for the rarer rectangular pin/ashtray.

The Royal Torquay Pottery, successor to the Torquay Terracotta Company at Hele Cross, also made commemorative mugs for the Silver Jubilee – indeed, these are the only Royal commemoratives the Company is known to have made and even these are rarely found. Two versions have been seen, on either a blue or a cream gound, although they are identical in style (fig. 18). The bust of the King and Queen are in relief and are most unusual in that both are crowned; the inscription on the reverse is simply 'Silver Jubilee 1910 to 1935'. These commemoratives do not have a pottery backstamp, but are easily recognisable because of the crowned heads and because, like most of Royal Torquay's output, they are heavily potted and rather crudely decorated.

The most artistic of all the Torquay Pottery's Jubilee commemoratives must be those made by the Longpark Pottery. These are decorated with a

Fig. 18. Selection of items made for the Silver Jubilee in 1935. The two mugs with applied sprigged heads wearing crowns were made by the Royal Torquay Pottery. The two beakers are decorated with an Alexandra rose and sponged mauve borders; they were made by Longpark. The mug at the bottom right is transfer decorated and was made at the Bovey Pottery Co. Ltd. Other mugs by Watcombe.

pink Alexandra rose and have mauve sponged bands at the base and rim. They are usually inscribed 'Royal Silver Jubilee May 6th 1935' and sometimes also carry place ,or personal names. Many of these were distributed to children in Kingskerswell at their Jubilee party. So far, only beakers have been seen, although these come in two sizes (4 inches and 4¹/₂ inches) and some have matching saucers.

Coronation 1937

Less than a year after the Jubilee celebrations, King George V had died and was succeeded by his son, who became King Edward VIII. As the Prince of Wales, Edward had been extremely popular with the public, partly because as a 'modern royal' he had travelled extensively to working class areas especially during the Depression. Preparations were well under way for his Coronation on May 12th 1937, including the manufacture of souvenirs, when a constitutional crisis arose over the King's wish to marry an American divorcee, Mrs. Wallis Simpson. Parliament would not sanction the marriage – as head of the Church of England the Monarch must be seen to uphold its beliefs – and so King Edward abdicated on 10th December 1936. The King's younger brother, Albert, Duke of York, succeeded him as King George VI, and decided his Coronation would go ahead on the same date.

The Watcombe and Longpark Potteries had already produced many commemoratives for the Coronation of Edward VIII when he abdicated and some of these were shown in the

Fig. 19. Items made for the Coronation of King Edward VIII and his Abdication. Left to right: transfer printed mug made by the Bovey Pottery Co.; Watcombe mug inscribed on the reverse 'Torquay Town Council'; two Watcombe tapering beakers with handles, both have the same sprigged heads but the one on the left is for the Coronation whilst that on the right has been converted to 'A Souvenir of the Abdication'. Two mugs in the front with the 'Coronation' head surrounded by blue and mauve lines to make Abdication souvenirs, both by Watcombe; beaker by Longpark decorated with the Alexandra rose pattern for the Coronation – none of these have been seen converted to Abdication souvenirs.

Fig. 20. *Boer War commemoratives: terracotta plaques by Watcombe, all other items by Aller Vale. Top row, left to right: double handled waisted mug decorated with the scandy pattern and a sprigged head of Baden-Powell and the scouting motto; five 'Tommy Atkins' commemoratives; jug decorated with a scandy pattern and the scouting motto but no head of Baden-Powell. Bottom row: jug commemorating the Jameson Raid; terracotta plaque with head of Lieut. Gen. Sir George White; miniature tyg with crossed flags of the U.K. and South Africa; plate decorated with flowers and leaves and the motto 'Have courage boys to do the right' etc. which was popular for several years after the Boer War was over; terracotta plaque with head of Lord Kitchener; two handled mug with Tommy Atkins motto.*

Torquay Herald Express of 12th December 1936 (fig. 24). Longpark had decided to repeat their Alexandra rose design which had proved popular for the Silver Jubilee. The Watcombe Pottery produced a new design which was decorated with the head of Edward and a crown in relief surrounded by national plants of thistles, roses and shamrocks – a modern version of their 1911 and 1902 commemoratives; 'Coronation of Edward VIII May 1937' is in s'graffito on a swag underneath the head. The decoration is very artistic and was the work of Reginald Wilson, one of Watcombe's best decorators. Some of these mugs have been seen inscribed on the re-verse 'Torquay Town Council May 1937'; however there is no evidence that the Council commissioned these mugs at all so they were probably made as samples in the hope of securing an order! Torquay Town Council gave beakers made by the Bovey Pottery to local schoolchildren. Beakers were also made with a plainer decoration of a laurel wreath surrounding the head and an inscription 'Long may he reign'. When Edward VIII abdicated Watcombe converted some of their Coronation commemoratives to 'A Souvenir of the Abdication' the same head sprigs were used but surrounded by sombre red and blue lines or a laurel wreath instead of the patri-

Fig. 21. Reginald Wilson at Watcombe in the late 1940's. He was one of Watcombe's top decorators, and designed the sprigs for the 1937 and 1953 commemoratives.

otic flowers (fig. 19). Abdication commemoratives are rare and are highly sought by collectors.

Watcombe produced a new design for the Coronation of George VI and Queen Elizabeth and this shows their two heads in relief surrounded by laurel leaves; they are even rarer then Abdication mugs! More common are the pin/ashtrays which are combination Coronation and holiday souvenirs; they are decorated with a standard Art Deco design and are inscribed 'A memento of a visit to the Lake District and the Coronation of King George VI 1937'.

Although the products of the Bovey Tracey Pottery are not considered to be 'Torquay Pottery' many collectors like to have a few examples because of the local connection. The Bovey Pottery made slip cast wares with transfer printed decorations and, although many of them are attractive, they lack the rustic charm of the hand-decorated Torquay pieces.

Fig. 22. Beakers made by the Longpark Pottery. The one on the left was made for the Silver Jubilee in 1935, on the right for the 'Coronation of King Edward VIII May 12th 1937'.

Fig. 23. Reverse of No. 22.

FROM *THE POTTERY GAZETTE*

December 1st 1936 – Editorial Notes.

'At first it is a little hard to believe that articles which might be sold as mementoes of the Coronation of King Edward VIII could have their origin in a foreign country. . . . It is apalling to think that a Coronation mug given by a British school to a British child as a souvenir of the Coronation of a British King should have been made by other than British hands . . . Such thoughts have troubled the Import Duties Advisory Committee, and so they recommended to the Treasury that duty of 100 per cent should be levied on all foreign goods likely to be used as souvenirs of King Edward's Coronation. The Treasury have accepted the recommendation and the duty will come into force on December 15th and will remain until July 31st, 1937.

Fig. 24. Photograph which appeared in the 'Torquay Herald and Express' 12th December 1936. The large vases were decorated with applied flowers and leaves under an amber glaze and are an example of Longpark Art Pottery; they are inscribed on the base 'Made at Longpark Torquay, October 24th 1936, Frederick H. Blackler, Managing Director'.

Fig. 25. Commemoratives made for the Coronation of King George VI and Queen Elizabeth 1937. Left and right: beakers by Longpark decorated with an Alexandra rose; mug with sprigged heads by Watcombe; transfer printed mug by Bovey Pottery Co.; ashtray or pintray by Watcombe is a double commemorative for the Coronation and a souvenir of a visit to the Lake District.

Coronation of H.M. Queen Elizabeth II 1953

When King George VI came to the throne Europe was on the threshold of war; restrictions imposed by the Board of Trade in 1942 forbade the production of decorated wares, except for export, and these restrictions lasted until 1952. Of the old Torquay Potteries, only Watcombe and Longpark survived into the post-war world, the latter being reduced to the production of popular mottowares and not much else. Reginald Wilson was still at the Watcombe Pottery and he produced a new design for the 1953 Coronation of Queen Elizabeth II who came to the throne on the death of her father on 6th February 1952. These commemoratives show the head of the Queen surrounded by a frame of laurel leaves and with the simple inscription 'E II R 1953'. Two versions of mugs have been seen, on cream or blue grounds, and also dressing table trays (fig. 27); sometimes the laurel leaves are in yellow.

After the War several new potteries sprang up in South Devon making pottery using local clays and traditional techniques and of these, the Dartmouth and Sandygate Potteries made 1953 Coronation commemoratives. The Dartmouth Pottery was started in 1948 and recruited the services of Mr.Leo Lewis, a modeller-mouldmaker from North Staffordshire, who designed their Coronation wares – his designs were shown at the British Industries Fair in 1952. The commemoratives show a white head of the Queen under a crown with a

Fig. 26. Military commemoratives, World War II and after. On the left three figures from the 'Our Gang' series by Bovey Pottery Co. The cream version (Roosevelt) was made for the home market as government restrictions prevented the production of decorated wares for the home market. The soldier and Winston Churchill must have been made for export. Vase in the centre, eight inches (20 cms.) tall made by Watcombe and decorated with an R.A.F. eagle, inscribed on the reverse '26/6/40 M.L.'. The pint mugs on the right are decorated with badges for the Red Cross, R.E.M.E., and R.A.F.; most were decorated by Reginald Wilson and sold to American servicemen.

Fig. 27. Selection of items made for the 1953 Coronation of Queen Elizabeth II. Left to right, back row: Dartmouth plate with cream sprigs on a brown ground under an amber glaze, Watcombe beaker, blue ground; Watcombe dressing table tray, blue; Dartmouth jug; Dartmouth plate, blue with additional inscription 'Royal visit to New Zealand 1953'. Front row, left to right: Sandygate mug, sprigged decoration on pale blue ground; Dartmouth mug; Watcombe beaker, cream ground; Dartmouth mug; Sandygate mug with official transfer design on pale turquoise ground.

scroll inscription: 'Elizabeth R June 1953' all done in relief on a dark brown mottled ground and under an amber glaze (fig. 27). Sometimes a wreath of laurel surrounds the head and on jugs, tankards etc. the Royal Coat of Arms also appears on the reverse. A great variety of items were made as commemoratives, including pint and half pint tankards, plates, jugs and teapots; they are most attractive! The same design was used for blue and white slip cast wares to commemorate Queen Elizabeth's visit to New Zealand in 1953.

The Sandygate Pottery at Kingsteignton also made commemorative mugs for Queen Elizabeth II's Coronation – some of these were decorated with the official transferred design of the Royal Coat of Arms which was used for many different souvenirs, especially those given to children – some Sandygate pieces have been seen with 'Chichester' stamped on the base but no other pottery marks. More unusual, though, are the commemoratives with heads of the Monarch done in relief – they are typically on a blue or turquoise background.

During the 1960's the Watcombe Pottery closed and other South Devon Potteries gave up making Torquay type wares in favour of cheaper slip cast wares. Some of these made commemoratives and although many are attractive, they have little appeal to the Torquay Pottery collectors and are therefore outside the scope of this book.

Fig. 28. Leo Lewis with his model of the Coronation mug designed for Dartmouth Pottery. Photograph from The Pottery Gazette July 1952 reproduced by permission of Dartmouth Pottery.

FROM *THE POTTERY GAZETTE*

June 1st 1952

DARTMOUTH POTTERY: Report of British Industries Fair, Earls Court, London.

'The new Coronation brown and honey coloured mugs were also much in evidence and brought forth many enquiries'.

August 1952.

The President of the Board of Trade has stated that import of Coronation souvenirs from foreign countries is prohibited.

January 1953.

'News' reported that
'. . . the Treasury had made an order giving temporary relief from Purchase Tax made on Coronation souvenirs'.

Mottoes

We therefore have great cause of
thankfulness.

See! Victoria's Glorious Reign
How England does it's best attain
Because thro' Sixty years she's been
Our Great our Good our Gracious
1837   Queen   1897

Prince Edward of York 1894
Bright be the stars on the eve of St.
John
Luckie the babe that is born thereon
(Aller Vale tyg).

Borough of Poole
To commemorate the coronation
of their majesties
King George V and Queen Mary
22 June 1911
L. D. Ballard
Mayor

MILITARY COMMEMORATIVES

The British have been a great seafaring and trading nation for many centuries and, as such, have often been engaged in battles to protect their overseas interests. Victories were widely, and often wildly, celebrated and, by the early nineteenth century, these events were subjects for the growing commemorative market. Trafalgar, Nelson's death, the Crimean War were extensively commemorated, showing Britain's glory and power in the world. Towards the end of the century, the 'Scramble for Africa' was under way and the public's great enthusiasm for the Sudan campaign, and the struggle for the control of South Africa resulted in a huge output of memorabilia recording these events.

Gordon of Khartoum

The public's great hero of the early 1880's was General Gordon and his death at the hands of the Mahdi in 1885 was commemorated by both the Watcombe and Aller Vale Potteries. Gordon was a veteran of the Crimean and Chinese Wars before being invited by the Khedive of Egypt to become Governor of Southern Sudan. During his six years there he conquered and pacified a huge area of over a million square miles before ill health forced him to return to England in 1880. However, within three years a rebellion, led by a Muslim fanatic known as the Mahdi, threatened to destabilise the Sudan. The public clamoured for Gordon to be sent to restore order and eventually the Prime Minister, Gladstone, responded to their demands and despatched Gordon to evacuate Egyptian forces and withdraw from Khartoum. Gordon, though, was determined to crush the rebel forces first, which delayed the evacuation of the town.

Rebels encircled the town and the siege began. Gladstone was reluctant to send a relief party, believing Gordon had over-reached his authority, but pressure from the public forced him to do so. They reached Khartoum on 28th January 1885 to find they were two days too late as Khartoum had fallen, after a siege of 317 days, and Gordon killed as he stood at the top of the palace steps. The public blamed Gladstone and his ministers for their apathy and proclaimed Gordon a 'martyred warrior saint'.

Fig. 29. Reverse of small bust of Gordon to show details of sculptor and manufacturer.

The East and South Devon Advertiser extolled Gordon's achievements on 7th February 1885 (before news of his death reached England): 'Among so many heroes Gordon is the most eminent and most revered. . . . For an entire year he has, by his splendid genius, his commanding character, his unflinching resolution, his inexhaustible resources, kept the wild fanaticism of the desert at bay. There is no other way of doing justice to his qualities and achievements than by saying he is a King of Men'. When four days later, news reached those readers of the death of their hero, what more natural than that they should purchase a commemorative made by the local potteries to honour his memory. Aller Vale adapted their standard Kerswell Daisy pattern tygs by adding an appropriate inscription in s'graffito (fig. 30).

'Gordon Kartoum 26.1.85
At all times, and everywhere, he gave
his strength to the weak, his substance
to the poor, his sympathy to the suffering,
his heart to God'.

Note the incorrect spelling of Khartoum! Errors such as these are one of the endearing qualities of Torquay Pottery – after all, at the end of a hard day anyone can make mistakes!

Fig. 30. Commemoratives in memory of Gordon of Khartoum. Left to right: Aller Vale loving cup decorated with the Kerswell Daisy pattern under an amber glaze; note the incorrect spelling of 'Kartoum'! terracotta bust of General Gordon nine and a half inches (24 cms.) tall excluding socle, unmarked but probably Watcombe; small terracotta bust of Gordon modelled by W. C. Lawton for the Watcombe Pottery; contemporary line drawing of Gordon in terracotta frame made by the Torquay Terracotta Company.

The Watcombe Pottery produced two versions of terracotta busts depicting the General. The smaller one is just four and a half inches tall and was sculpted by W.C.Lawton; the detailing is superb and shows Gordon in full military splendour. The reverse is inscribed with the name of the pottery, the sculptor and impressed numbers 685 which are date marks – the 6 denotes the six month (June) and 85 the year 1885. (fig. 29). The larger bust of Gordon is much coarser in style and shows the General in typical headgear of a fez. Although this bust carried no backstamp, it is almost certainly from the Watcombe Pottery.

South Africa and the Boer War

A decade after the fall of Khartoum, Britain was being slowly drawn into conflict in Southern Africa which culminated in the Boer War of 1899-1902, an event which spawned more Torquay commemoratives than all the other military events put together.

Fig. 31. Aller Vale jug, six and a quarter inches (16 cms.) tall commemorating the Jameson Raid. Decorated in Kerswell Daisy pattern.

Gold was discovered in the Transvaal in the 1880's and this brought in huge numbers of prospectors from British South Africa; these people were known as 'Uitlanders' and they suffered discrimination from the President of Transvaal, Paul Kruger, and his Boer government. In December 1895 some of the Uitlanders organised an uprising, encouraged by Cecil Rhodes, Governor of neighbouring British South Africa. This gave Dr. L. Storr Jameson, one of Rhodes' close associates, the excuse he wanted to lead a force of 470 men into the Transvaal with the aim of overthrowing Kruger's government. The conspiracy failed and Jameson's force was captured within four days. To the British public at home, though, Jameson was seen as a hero seeking to protect the rights of Uitlanders, and the Aller Vale commemorative jugs (fig. 31)

present him in this light, as can be seen by the inscription:

Here's to our brave, our Dr. Jim
  South Afrie's hero true
Who counting not, nor life, nor limb
  Swift to the rescue flew.

Although Jameson's Raid failed, the Uitlanders continued to press the British government to take action against the oppressive Boer government. Eventually their protests grew so loud that the Boers decided the only way to settle the issue was to declare war on the British, which they did in October 1899. Initially the British thought defeating the Boers would be easy as they had no regular army but this proved to be far from true; after a series of disasters the British were confronted with a guerilla war which was not won until May 1902.

31

A huge variety of commemoratives were made by Aller Vale and Watcombe to celebrate victories and personalities in the Boer War. The most common of all Torquay Pottery commemoratives are those made by Aller Vale showing the figure of Tommy Atkins done in relief. These invariably carry the inscription 'God Bless you Tommy Atkins Here's your country's love to you' and the date 1899–1900. These commemoratives were issued following the Relief of Mafeking when, it was generally believed, the War was all but over. Mafeking was relieved on 17th May 1900 after a siege of seven months; news of this Victory was greeted with great joy by the British public. Newton Abbot was typical of many towns and the Newton News of June 1900 reported that 'some hundreds of people soon gathered in the streets, and 'God Save the Queen' and 'Soldiers of the Queen' were sung by the crowd at the Tower'. A grand procession and carnival was arranged at a few hours notice and it was estimated that 'between three and four thousand people' visited the festivities in Courtnay Park. Within two or three weeks towns and villages had set up committees to arrange celebrations pending the imminent signing of a Peace Treaty. However, the War dragged on another two painful years by which time the British were grateful simply to have won a victory!

Thousands of Boer War commemoratives were made by different potteries but the motif of a soldier in khaki is unusual – far more depict generals, flags or particular regiments. The Torquay Peace Committee had proposed setting up a fund to pay for a statue of a soldier to be erected in the town; although the statue never materialised, it is possible that the Aller Vale commemoratives are connected with this proposal. Tommy Atkins was the

Fig. 32. Aller Vale Boer War mug with applied sprig of a soldier in khaki known as 'Tommy Atkins'.

name chosen to show potential recruits how to fill in forms to join the army at the end of the Napoleonic War. Tommy Atkins was believed to have fought under Wellington and lost his life in 1794 during the Netherlands Campaign. The name stuck as a generic term to describe a private in the British Army and was popularised by Kipling (a Boer War correspondent) in his poem 'Tommy'.

The Aller Vale Tommy Atkins commemoratives were made in a variety of styles and sizes ranging from miniature loving cups one and three quarter inches tall to three handled tygs and jugs up to five inches tall. Some of these are shown in fig. 20. A more unusual Tommy Atkins tyg consisted of bands of brown, white and blue slip with just a motto – the only form of embellishment is in the moulded handles.

Fig. 33. Watcombe terracotta wall plaque seven inches (18 cms.) tall, moulded in relief with a bust of Lieutenant-General Sir George White, V.C., G.C.B. The oil painted chrysanthemums were a popular decoration on a variety of terracotta items in the late 1890's.

plaques have been painted in oils with chrysanthemums or roses, which were standard decorations at the time. The figures are not named and are often difficult to identify but those seen are believed to commemorate Lieutenant-General Sir George White, (see fig. 33) and Lord Kitchener.

Collectors should also look out for miniature tygs with crossed flags of Britain and South Africa which have the motto 'Each of them doing their country's work, South Africa 1899–1900'. The crossed flag motif was later used by Aller Vale for similar tygs commemorating America's entry in World War I.

In addition to commemoratives, the Torquay Potteries inscribed many of their standard mottowares with

The hero of Mafeking was Baden Powell, who was promoted to Major-General on account of his gallantry and leadership during the Siege. Aller Vale made commemoratives decorated with the portrait of Baden Powell with his signature and the well known scouting motto which is the reverse of the Black Warrior's Song:

'If we go forward we die
If we go backward, we die
Better go forward and die'

The Watcombe Pottery made wall plaques depicting heads of Generals although these, like the Aller Vale Baden Powell tygs, are hard to find. The Watcombe pieces are moulded in terracotta, roughly heart shaped with a fluted edge. The heads of the military chiefs are done in relief and framed with a horseshoe. Sometimes the

---

Article in *COUNTRY LIFE ILLUSTRATED*

March 9th 1901 on 'Aller Vale Pottery'.

'When I visited the works the war fever was at its height, and the walls in the decorators' room were adorned with pictures of General Roberts, General Buller, and other popular favourites. On a three handled loving-cup was a picture of Baden-Powell, with his signature and the well-known scouting motto – the reverse of the Black Warrior's song:

If we go forward, we die,
If we go backward, we die
Better go backward and die.

Note: Although this is the verse quoted in Country Life Illustrated, all the Baden-Powell commemoratives that have been seen have the last line as:

Better go forward and die.

patriotic verses – one of the most popular verse was:

'Have courage boys to do the right
Be bold be brave be strong
By doing right you gain the might
To overcome the wrong'.

These mottoes were used for several years after the Boer War was over and have appeared on items made by Aller Vale, Watcombe and Longpark.

World War I

The start of World War I in 1914 was greeted with much enthusiasm by the British public yet surprisingly few commemoratives were made by the Torquay Potteries for this event. Watcombe made tobacco jars and jugs decorated in pigment underglaze with the flags of the Allies – Britain, France, Russia and Belgium – and the motto 'United we stand 1914' around the flags. Sometimes another motto such as 'May the hinges of friendship never go rusty' appeared on the reverse. These items are quite rare and are eagerly sought by collectors (fig. 34).

The flag motif was again used by Aller Vale to commemorate the entry of the U.S.A. into World War I in April 1917. The flags are the Union Jack and the Stars and Stripes and above the flags is the motto 'May they ever be united'. Some of those commemoratives have clasped hands underneath the flags, a motif that had previously been popular during the Crimean War! So far, only small tygs have been seen decorated in this way. In spite of their small size, just one and three quarter inches tall, they

Fig. 34. World War I commemoratives. Back row: four regimental commemoratives made by the Royal Torquay Pottery, left to right: Devons bowl, Royal Engineers jug, Royal Army Medical Corps jug, Devons chalice. Front row: left to right: Watcombe jug with Allied flags in 1914 – Britain, France, Russia and Belgium; two small loving cups by Aller Vale with crossed flags of U.S.A. and Britain to commemorate America's entry into the War in 1917; Devons jug and A.S.C. jug by Royal Torquay. The Greetings card with an A.S.C. badge is signed 'From Billy'. R.A.M.C. jug five inches (12.5 cms) tall.

have rather a long motto scratched on the reverse:

'Our hearts our hopes
Our prayers, our tears
Our faith triumphant
o'er our fears
Are all with thee'.

Collectors may come across jugs, bowls, etc. which have applied regimental badges – they are undated and do not have any pottery backstamp to indicate their source. A selection of these is shown in fig. 34. These items almost certainly originate from the Royal Torquay Pottery at Hele Cross. The products of this Pottery tend to be 'chunky' and the decoration is coarser than on pieces from Aller Vale, Watcombe or Longpark. These regimental wares were made during World War I as is evidenced by their simple mottoes such as 'England expects', 'United we stand', or 'Our friends all love, our foes all fear you'. The most common of these commemoratives are, quite naturally, for the local regiment the 'Devons'; others have been seen for the R.A.M.C., R.E., and A.S.C., but possibly more will come to light. A wide variety of items were made; jugs and sugar bowls are the most common, but collectors should look for the rarer chalice shaped cream bowls and teapots.

Once the War was over towns and villages began to think in terms of peace celebrations that would be appropriate – i.e. to show people's joy that the War was over, whilst paying due reverence to the dead and injured. An added complication was that the Government declined to designate an official Victory Day until the Peace Treaties were signed. Rumours abounded that it would be the first Sunday in August and the succeeding two days (it was already a Bank Holi-

Fig. 35. 'Devons' regimental jug two and a half inches (6.5 cms.) tall by Royal Torquay. The moulded badges are often crudely done. The motto on the reverse is 'Doing their duty'.

day weekend) and many towns settled on those dates. However, after the Treaty of Versailles had been signed on 28th June 1919 the Government then announced Victory Day would be Saturday 19th July – less than three weeks away! This caused great confusion with some towns moving their events forward to the 19th July whilst others kept to the Bank Holiday weekend.

In Torquay the plans for their Peace Celebrations caused a local 'war' between the Council and townspeople. An original proposal that £2,000 should be taken from the rates to pay for an elaborate pageant met with a barrage of protests from the residents that such a huge sum of ratepayers' money should be frittered away. After that, the Mayor and Corporation took umbrage and did nothing! An editorial in the Torquay Times of 18th July was vociferous in its criticism of the Mayor and Council, blaming them for lack of leadership which resulted in a 'meagre, poverty stricken programme, which is put in the shade by a dozen little Devonshire hamlets'. The criticism was perhaps a little unjust because, little more than a week before Victory Day, some local tradesmen had formed a committee and raised funds to put on a modest parade, sports and teas for 4,000 local children. In the event there was a torrential downpour on Saturday the 19th July and most of the festivities had to be postponed or cancelled!

The 'little Devonshire hamlets' (now suburbs of Torquay!) had their festivities in August – at Barton they took place on Saturday 2nd and at Hele, St.Marychurch on Wednesday 6th. The sun shone both days – no doubt to the smug satisfaction of the writer in the 'Torquay Times' who commented that Hele 'put aristocratic, wealthy, populous Torquay to shame' with its 'gorgeous little peace celebration' consisting of parades, hymn singing, sports and a 'sumptuous tea' for 'the kiddies, the service men and the old age pensioners'.

The Barton celebrations were much the same but it had been decided to give the children a commemorative made by the nearby Watcombe Pottery to remember the occasion. The Torquay Times informed its readers '. . . it is the intention to present each Barton child with a commemoration mug with a suitable inscription. Owing to unforeseen circumstances these could not be prepared in time.'! They were later distributed through the schools to some 80 children.

St. Marychurch gave its children similar mugs made by Watcombe; they were all decorated with the 'scandy' pattern which was a popular mottoware line. The children had to assemble at the Chilcote Memorial, St.Marychurch, to be presented with their mugs by a local dignatory!

At St. Budeaux, near Plymouth, children were given similar scandy mugs made by the Longpark Pottery, inscribed 'St. Budeaux Peace Celebrations Aug. 4th 1919'. Longpark can be distinguished from Watcombe or Aller Vale because the lettering is typically much broader with distinctive curly 'e's'. The St. Budeaux celebrations were much bigger than those at Barton or St. Marychurch,

Fig. 36. Mugs to celebrate the Peace in 1919. Left to right: Watcombe mug inscribed 'Barton 1919 Peace Celebration'; St. Budeaux mug by Longpark; St.Marychurch mug by Watcombe. All are decorated with the scandy pattern which was a popular design for mottowares.

and consequently those commemoratives are easier to find. The celebrations took place at St. Budeaux Naval Rest Camp and 2,000 children sat down to tea.

The Great War had brought the age of Imperialism to an end and militarism went into a decline. Few commemoratives were made and those that were, are more in the style of gifts or souvenirs, for instance a mug inscribed 'With the Devonport Petty Officers Best Wishes for 1932' was presumably a Christmas or New Year gift! These mugs are very plain (fig. 37) and were made at the Devon Tors Pottery at Bovey Tracey. Longpark added an 'icing' type inscription 'H.M.S. Apollo' to their standard mugs decorated with a diving Kingfisher on a blue gound.

World War II

When War broke out again in 1939 there was no public jubilation, simply a determination to defeat the enemy. The introduction of a war economy meant that restrictions had to be placed on non-essential goods and this applied to certain categories of china. The Domestic Pottery Order of 1942 banned the manufacture of decorated china for the home market although it was permitted on exported goods; the ban remained in force until well after the War was over.

Military commemoratives made during the War are often of the personal type, such as a vase decorated with an eagle and inscribed on the back '26/6/40 M.L.' (fig. 26). This is believed to have been made for someone joining the R.A.F. possibly one of the potters, as about half the pottery trade workers were called up to do National Service. Another personal souvenir is a Watcombe plaque six and a quarter inches in diameter, dec-

Fig. 37. Yellow vase, three and threequarter inches (9.5 cms.) tall inscribed 'With the Devonport Petty Officer's Best Wishes for 1932'. The obverse is decorated with windmills done in brown pigments under a clear glaze.

orated with a black Spitfire and the motto 'Never was so much owed by so many to so few'; on the base is written 'Made and decorated by Robert G. Fry 1942' (fig. 38). The quotation comes from a speech made by the Prime Minister Winston Churchill to the House of Commons on 20th August 1940 in praise of R.A.F. pilots during the Battle of Britain.

The Torquay Potteries had always exported widely – to the Dominions and Colonies, as well as to the U.S.A. – and some of these wares included commemoratives. The Watcombe Pottery produced small rectangular pin/ashtrays inscribed 'Remember Pearl Harbor' and 'doll sized' globular teapots and jugs with 'V for Victory' – although not common they turn up at antique shops in the U.S.A. occasionally.

Fig. 38. Watcombe plaque, six and a quarter inches (16 cms.) diameter, decorated in pigments with a deep pink border and black Spitfire. Inscribed on the reverse 'Made and decorated by Robert G. Fry 1942'.

Many collectors of Torquay Pottery like to have examples of the 'Our Gang' series of figures made by the Bovey Pottery Co.Ltd., to add to their collection of commemoratives. The most common figures are 'The Big Three', Roosevelt, Churchill and Stalin, but in addition to these some fourteen other models were made of soldiers, sailors, airmen, nurses etc. An advertisement in the Pottery Gazette of March 1941 also showed models of Hitler and Mussolini but these cannot have been popular – unless, of course, to be smashed to pieces, which would account for their rarity today! All the figures were eight inches tall and were sculpted by Gwynneth Holt and Fenton Wyness; they are monotoned, usually cream or mustard, although some coloured examples have been seen – probably made for export! (fig. 26). One example of a sergeant major has been seen with a pale green glaze.

The continuation of Wartime restrictions meant that no commemoratives could be made for the offical Victory Day Celebrations on June 8th 1946. The pottery trade complained about this, as did local councils, but the Board of Trade were emphatic that they 'could not grant any temporary concessions for June 8th Celebrations'. However, in spite of this, some commemoratives were made although they are extremely rare! One was a mug, three inches tall, decorated with a cottage which was inscribed 'Glen Drive Victory Celebration 1945': these were given to children at a party in Stoke Bishop, Bristol, and each parent had to buy their own child's mug. Glen Drive obviously had their own Victory Celebrations well before the official day. The Devonmoor Pottery at Liverton also made Victory commemoratives to be given to children – these were in the form of a beaker, plain white with an orange V, and were given to some children in the Torquay area (fig. 39).

During the late 1940s Watcombe made a series of pint mugs with painted badges of regiments and other organisations such as the Red Cross (fig. 26). These pieces are usually personalised with the addition of initals or a name. The mugs were decorated by Reginald Wilson and were apparently particularly liked by American servicemen – American collectors should look out for them as they are rare!

Fig. 39. Two mugs celebrating the Victory in 1945. Left: Watcombe mug decorated with a cottage, inscribed 'Glen Drive Victory Celebration 1945' – Glen Drive was at Stoke Bishop near Bristol. Right: Devonmoor mug painted with a bright orange 'V' for Warbro Road, Babbacombe near Torquay. Both mugs are 'illegal' since government wartime restrictions banned the production of any decorated wares for the home market. The Devonmoor mug is four inches (10 cms.) tall.

Mottoes on regimental pots:

Doing their duty.

For England, Home and Beauty.

For the dear Homeland.

United we stand.

Your friends all love
Your foes all fear you.

England expects.

Mottoes

At all times and everywhere he gave
    his strength to the weak, his
    substance to the poor, his
    sympathy to the suffering, his
    heart to God.
Gordon Kartoum 26-1-85.
(Aller Vale tyg).

Here's to our brave our Dr. Jim
South Afrie's hero true
Who counting not, nor life nor limb
Swift to the rescue flew.
(Jug commemorating the Jameson
    Raid).

Some notable Royal and State events which may help in identifying Commemoratives

1871   Princess Louise, daughter of Queen Victoria, married the Marquis of Lorne (became Duke of Argyll in 1874).

1877   Queen Victoria declared Empress of India.

1885   Death of General Gordon at Khartoum. Princess Beatrice, daughter of Queen Victoria, married Prince Henry of Battenberg.

1887   Golden Jubilee of Queen Victoria's accession to the throne.

1888   Silver Wedding of the Prince and Princess of Wales (later King Edward VII and Queen Alexandra).

1892   Death of Duke of Clarence, eldest son of the Prince of Wales.

1893   Duke of York, second son of the Prince of Wales, married Victoria Mary (May) of Teck. They later became King George V and Queen Mary.

1894   Birth of Prince Edward of York, later King Edward VIII.

1897   Diamond Jubilee of Queen Victoria's accession to the throne.

1899–1902   Boer War. 1900: Relief of Kimberley, Ladysmith and Mafeking.

1901   Queen Victoria died on 22nd January.

1902   Coronation of King Edward VII and Queen Alexandra.

1910   King Edward VII died on 6th June.

1911   Coronation of King George V and Queen Mary. Investiture of the Prince of Wales at Caernarvon.

1914–1918   Great World War. 1917 U.S.A. entered Great War on side of Allies (Britain, France, Russia etc.) 1919 Peace Treaties signed.

1935   Silver Jubilee of King George V and Queen Mary.

1936   King George V died 20th January and was succeeded by King Edward VIII, who abdicated in December in favour of his younger brother who became King George VI.

1937   Coronation of King George VI and Queen Elizabeth.

1939–1945   World War Two. 1941 U.S.S.R. and U.S.A. entered war on side of Allies (Britain, France, etc.). 1946 Official Peace celebrations.

1951   Festival of Britain.

1952   King George VI died on 6th February.

1953   Coronation of Queen Elizabeth II and Prince Philip.

Royal commemoratives with place names

Many town or parish councils ordered commemoratives to be presented to children and often these were inscribed with a place name, or the name of a benefactor. Those that are known to exist are listed below, although possibly others may have been made.

1897	*Diamond Jubilee* Horton, Bucks (Aller Vale).
1902	*Coronation of King Edward VII and Queen Alexandra* St. John the Baptist, Cookham Dean (Watcombe). Donhead St. Mary (Aller Vale). Town and Hamlets, Holsworthy (Watcombe). Mrs. Mannings gift to Morwenstow (Watcombe). Parish of Pancrassweek (Watcombe). St. Catherine's, Sedgehill (Aller Vale). St. Margaret's, Sedgehill (Aller Vale). Borough of Shaftesbury (Aller Vale). St. Nicholas, Shaldon (Aller Vale).
1909	Visit by Prince and Princess of Wales to Chewton Mendip (Watcombe).
1911	*Coronation of King George V and Queen Mary* St. John the Baptist, Cookham Dean (Aller Vale). Denston (Watcombe).

Lyndhurst (Watcombe).
Lytchett Matravers (Crown Dorset).
Minstead (Watcombe).
Borough of Poole (Crown Dorset).
Shaldon (Watcombe).
Sturminster Marshall (Crown Dorset).

| 1935 | *Silver Jubilee of King George V and Queen Mary*
Kingskerswell (Longpark).
Walton on Naze (Watcombe). |
| 1937 | *Coronation of King Edward VIII*
Torquay Town Council (Watcombe). |

41

POLITICIANS AND POLITICAL CAUSES

Political commemoratives had grown in popularity during the nineteenth century with busts and figures of politicians, and mugs to celebrate elections. Both Watcombe and the Torquay Terracotta Company produced terracotta busts of popular politicians. Many of the Watcombe busts were modelled by W. C. Lawton and those include John Bright (1884) and the Marquis of Salisbury (1885). The small bust of Gladstone by A. Bruce Joy (1884) was copied from the head of the statue at The East End of London. The Torquay Terracotta Company also made busts of Gladstone but the sculptor is unknown; possibly it was Alfred Bentley as he sculpted their bust of John Bright, and is known to have worked at the Pottery for many years.

A much more controversial head of Gladstone was made by the Aller Vale pottery; this is in the form of a moulded jug with an axe for the handle resting against Gladstone's head (fig. 40). The jugs are made of white clay and are dipped in a green or straw coloured glaze. The design was registered at the Patent Office on 27th July 1885 and the Registration Number 30493 is impressed on the base of the jugs. Gladstone had become increasingly unpopular, both with the public and his own party, during his second Ministry 1880–85 because of his support for Irish Home Rule – to many Protestants 'Home Rule means Rome Rule' and they vigorously opposed it. The debacle over Khartoum in January 1885 increased Gladstone's problems (for a time the Grand Old Man was nicknamed Gordon's Own Murderer) and in June

he was forced to resign when Irish Nationalists, Conservatives and 70 rebels from within his own Liberal Party refused to support him on a vote of confidence. The Aller Vale jugs record this event. Gladstone was out of office for only six months but his subsequent attempts to 'solve' the Irish problem through Home Rule Bills in 1886 and 1893 both failed.

The Irish cause also featured on a small pot made by the Crown Dorset Pottery in Poole; it is so like Torquay Pottery in decoration that many collectors might mistake it for such (fig. 40). The shape was known as an owl pot although it is a small version of an old Dorset cider flask; a cord was threaded through the ring holes so that farm workers could hang the flask around their necks to quench their thirst when working in the fields. The pot is decorated with an orange flag with the cross of St. George in the corner; this is the Boyne Standard which is reputed to have been carried by the Williamite Army at the time of the Glorious Revolution in 1688. The pot was made as a commemorative to support Ulster's opposition to the Third Irish Home Rule Bill of 1912.

The Devon Tors Pottery made small round bowls as souvenirs of a very local political event, the May Day bazaar organised by Totnes Divisional Labour Party in 1926. The bazaar was held in Newton Abbot with the aim of raising funds for the Party and the principal guest of honour was Mr. George Lansbury, M. P. for Poplar. Mr. Lansbury's address centred around the crisis in the coal industry and was reported in the following

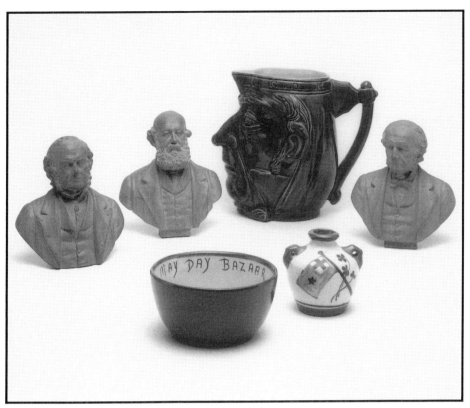

Fig. 40. Commemoratives with Political connections. Three terracotta busts made by Watcombe commemorating politicians: left to right: John Bright, sculpted by W. C. Lawton, the Marquis of Salisbury by Lawton, Gladstone by A. Bruce Joy. Face jug also of Gladstone by Aller Vale: this is made of white clay dipped in a green glaze; note the GOM (Grand Old Man) incised around the rim. Small bowl made by Devon Tors Pottery at Bovey Tracey for the May Day Bazaar organised by Totnes Divisional Labour Party in 1926. Small 'owl' pot made by the Crown Dorset Pottery, decorated with the Boyne Standard, and made to show Ulster's opposition to the Home Rule Bill of 1912. Gladstone face jug six inches (15 cms.) tall.

week's edition of the 'Mid-Devon and Newton Times', an issue much reduced in size due to the General Strike! The report noted 'A flower stand of pottery ware made at the Bovey Potteries, and suitably inscribed, was presented to Mr. Lansbury' – although the whereabouts of this piece (if it still exists) is unknown, the bowls can sometimes be found and they carry the simple inscription 'May Day Bazaar Newton Abbot 1926'.

FROM *THE POTTERY GAZETTE*

Dec. 1st 1903.
'The Watcombe Collection is also replete with art form and artistic treatment . . . There is a terracotta bust of Mr. Chamberlain and some very pretty terracotta groups'.

Commemoratives with a religious theme

The Torquay Potteries produced a great number of mottowares with religious or moral sayings etched on them and these were especially popular during the first quarter of the twentieth century. Commemoratives with a religious theme are much rarer and fall roughly into three categories: those with specifically religious verses, busts of church leaders and those which are souvenirs of religious events.

The Aller Vale Pottery made plates with devotional inscriptions, perhaps due to the influence of its owner, John Phillips, who was a regular worshipper at Abbotskerswell Church. The earliest of these is inscribed 'Motto for 1888: They dwelt with the King for his work I Crons. Chapter IV verse 25'. The attribution of this motto is incorrect because it comes from 1 Chronicles verse 23, not 25. This motto is particularly approriate because the complete verse is 'These were the potters, and those that dwelt among plants and hedges: there they dwelt with the King for his work'. The plate is rather heavily potted and the decoration crudely done – it was probably the work of one of the boys from the local Cottage Art Schools who worked at the Pottery.

Another crudely made Aller Vale plate was decorated with a biblical scene and has the s'graffito inscription 'Abbotskerswell Sunday School Christmas 1891 Feed my lambs'. The simple naive scene of Jesus the Shepherd with children is especially suitable as a gift for the Sunday School children.

The Watcombe Pottery's range of terracotta busts included some commemorating church leaders. W.C.Lawton modelled a small bust, six inches tall of John Clifford M.A.,LL.B., who was an evangelical Baptist Minister. The busts were first produced in 1887, the year before Clifford was appointed President of the Baptist Union. A larger bust, twelve inches tall, was produced of Cardinal Newman and was sculpted by H.McDowell (fig. 41). This is made of coarser clay than the smaller bust which would suggest it is of later date. Newman was created a Cardinal in 1879 and died in August 1890.

The Torquay Potteries also produced souvenir wares to commemorate religious events. These included tablewares made for the Eucharistic Congress of 1932, and pintrays for the Octocentenary of Exeter Cathedral in 1933.

The 31st International Eucharistic Congress took place in Dublin from June 20th–26th 1932 and over 20,000 people attended. The Congress was opened by the Papal Legate Cardinal Lauri, and over 30 nations were represented by prelates, priests and laity. A high altar was erected in Phoenix Park and in addition to the religious services there were meetings and social events such as garden parties. The Longpark Pottery made cups and saucers and egg-cups commemorating this event – they are decorated with shamrocks and inscribed 'Eucharistic Congress 1932'. Several of the Torquay Potteries exported shamrock mottowares to Ireland and it seems likely that these commemoratives were commissioned by a local store.

In 1933 Exeter Cathedral celebrated the 800th Anniversay of its dedication to St.Peter. The Festival took place between 24th June and 2nd July and included special services, six performances of a new religious drama called 'The Acts of St.Peter', an organ recital by Ernest Bullock of Westminster Abbey, concerts, an exhibition of church silver and a Mayor's Banquet. The Cathedral was floodlit at night and chairs were hired so that visitors could admire the illuminations – although apparently the Cathedral Chapter were worried that they would have to pay compensation if the chairs were damaged by rain!! Thousands of visitors came for the celebrations and the local shops saw the opportunity for extra trade! Colsons organised a special programme for centenary week which included late night opening, organising guided tours around the Cathedral and a rest and writing room. Their advertisement in the Exeter 'Express and Echo' of June 24th 1933 advised readers to 'Take home to your friends a souvenir from Colsons of Exeter' – some of these were pin or ashtrays with a finely drawn view of the West End of the Cathedral surrounded by a yellow sprayed border. They are impressed 'Watcombe Torquay England' on the back and also have a black painted inscription 'Colsons of Exeter'. Colsons closed in the 1970's

Fig. 41. Commemoratives with a religious theme. Centre back: terracotta bust of Cardinal Newman twelve and a half inches (31.5 cms.) tall including socle, unmarked but probably Watcombe. Two plates by Aller Vale, on the left for Abbotskerswell Sunday School, Christmas 1891; on right: Motto for 1888. Two rectangular ashtrays (or pin trays) by Watcombe: on left to commemorate the Sally Williams Charity administered by Christchurch Priory; on right to commemorate the Octocentenary celebrations at Exeter Cathedral in 1933. Cup and saucer, and egg cup to commemorate the Eucharistic Congress held in Dublin in 1932, made by the Longpark Pottery. Note the incorrect spelling of 'Eucaristic' on the cup!

after nearly 200 years, as an independent shop, but their High Street site now operates as 'Dingles' department store.

Collectors may come across items made by the Torquay Potteries with scenes of churches or even tombstones – the Rogers puzzle tomb at Christchurch was popular! Whilst some may have been issued as commemoratives, the vast majority were sold as souvenir wares and are therefore outside the scope of this book.

Miscellaneous events

There were numerous commemoratives made for small local events and some of these are shown in fig. 42. A few of these are undated, such as the plates and mugs inscribed 'Cullompton May Fair' – perhaps they were sold over several years! In other instances such as the four and a half inch Watcombe jug inscribed 'Old Folks Gathering 1924 With Best Wishes H. Ellis, Mayor' there is no indication where the event took place, although with research it would be possible to find out which town had a mayor in 1924 called H. Ellis!! Many towns held Christmas dinner parties for local old folk so it is very likely these were given out on such an occasion.

Perhaps the most intriguing of all local commemoratives is an Aller Vale mug decorated with a scandy pattern which has the inscription 'In memoriam Opening Ipplepen Water Works October 4th 1907'. A report of this event appeared in 'The Mid-Devon and Newton News' of October 5th 1907 and by all accounts it was a day of celebration, not least because it was the culmination of nine year's effort to give Ipplepen a pure water supply. The story began in February 1898

REPORT IN *THE MID DEVON AND NEWTON TIMES*

October 5th 1907 on the Opening of the Ipplepen Water Works.

'Each child was presented with a mug, made at the Aller Vale Potteries, and bearing the inscription 'In commemoration of the Ipplepen Waterworks, October 4th 1907'. The money for the mugs, and for the children's tea was raised by public subscription – about £9 being raised. Mrs. Cooke presented the mugs to the children, and the Rev. R. D. Cooke, in addressing the children at the close, stated that those who were unable to attend, through sickness, would be given a mug'.

---

when a request by Newton Abbot Rural District Council for a loan to build a new sewage works was turned down by the Local Government Board because 'the water supply of the parish was deficient and should be remedied without delay'. The Council therefore decided to improve the water supply and engaged the services of a water diviner, Mr. Gataker, and Messr. Isler & Co. who were water borers. The newspaper reported 'The boring was carried to great depth, and although there was little sign of water, such faith was placed in the diviner that the work was persevered with until 1900 when it was abandoned without satisfactory result'. The bill for this was nearly £500 and a dispute arose over who should pay it – in the end the Rural District Council paid the bulk, but only after the Local Government Board had intervened!

The Council then negotiated with Paignton Urban Council, who were seeking to build additional Water Works, and secured favourable terms to buy water from them to supply a new Ipplepen reservoir. Even then, it was five years before the work was complete so it is perhaps not surprising that the opening of Ipplepen Water Works, became a real cause for celebration! The parishioners had a general holiday and local dignitaries as well as schoolchildren went to inspect the new reservoir. The children sang the National Anthem and waved Union Jacks as Councillor Mr. Matthew Fortescue turned on the taps – the pressure was tested by fire appliances to the great excitement of all who witnessed the jets of water shooting well above the roof tops. With such a joyous occasion, the collector must wonder why the mugs are inscribed 'In memoriam'; perhaps the local paper holds a clue to the answer.

The report noted 'Each child was presented with a mug, made at the Aller Vale Potteries, and bearing the inscription 'In commemoration of the Ipplepen Water Works, October 4th 1907'. Does this mean the mugs have the wrong inscription, perhaps a verbal order stating 'in commemoration' was it incorrectly interpreted as 'in memoriam'? The two hundred or so children who received them must have been just as curious as the collector today.

One of the popular events in Newton Abbot was the annual festivities in aid of the local hospital; this took place at the end of June and activities were usually organised over a week culminating in a Carnival Day on a Saturday, which was known as Newton Abbot Hospital Saturday. A

Fig. 42. Commemorating local events. Centre: dressing table tray, two candlesticks and ringholder decorated with crocuses;' made by Longpark for Newton Abbot Hospital Saturday 1934 – this was a fund raising event to support the local hospital. On the left: 'Old Folks Gathering' jug made by Watcombe and decorated with ships; Aller Vale mug decorated with the scandy pattern to commemorate the opening of the Ipplepen Water Works in 1907; brown Aller Vale mug with piped inscription 'Ye Cullompton May Fayre'. On the right, Dartmouth moulded white clay mug and oval dish to commemorate the sailing of the 'Mayflower' in 1620; mug in pale blue and dish dark blue. These souvenir items are found with various dates, such as '1956', and were presumably changed from year to year to cater for the tourist trade.

special committee worked all year planning this event. The Longpark Pottery made a dressing table set decorated with the crocus pattern and inscribed 'N. A. Hospital Saturday 1934', which was probably given as a prize in one of the many competitions that were organised. In September 1934 the Committee handed over £475 to the hospital, quite a large sum in those days!

At national level, the Watcombe Pottery made small round wall plaques commemorating the Festival of Britain in 1951. These show the Festival logo done in relief and often picked out in colours, although some examples have been seen in plain terracotta. The wartime restrictions on decorated wares were still in force and these curtailed the manufacture of elaborate souvenirs.

Collectors may sometimes be lucky enough to come across souvenirs made by the Torquay Potteries to commemorate overseas events. Aller Vale made jugs decorated with the Kerswell Daisy pattern to commemorate the 300th Anniversary of the landing of the Pilgrims at Plymouth Rock, Massachusetts, U.S.A. This Anniversary occurred in 1920, which is quite late for the Kerswell Daisy pattern. The jugs are inscribed with the motto:

Freely drink and quench
   thy thirst
Here drank the Pilgrim
   Father's first.

This motto had been used earlier on similar pieces sold in the U.S.A., but the 1920 commemoratives can be distinguished because they are inscribed on the base 'A. S. Burbank, Pilgrim Book and Art Store, Plymouth, Mass.' This company were well known as publishers of postcards from the

Fig. 43. Watcombe plaque, five and a half inches (14 cms.) diameter, moulded with the 1951 Festival of Britain logo.

1890's to 1920's, and were the only publishers officially authorised to provide souvenir cards for the Pilgrim Tercentenary in 1920. They also sold many other souvenirs including the specially commissioned Aller Vale jugs.

Commemorating conferences

The interwar years saw a growth in conferences organised by trade organisations and many of these were accompanied by their own commemoratives as a souvenir for delegates. Conferences were usually held in seaside resorts and were a combination of business and social events. With the growing popularity of 'annual holidays' many people took their families along to the conference – this provided them with a relatively cheap holiday because often the social events were sponsored by manufac-turers, and towns frequently offered free tickets for buses, the pier and concerts as an incentive to attract conferences.

Torquay Council actively promoted the town as a suitable venue for conferences; a special hospitality fund was set aside to entertain visiting VIP's and this often included the presentation of commemoratives made by the local potteries. Examples of these include a Longpark covered pot for the Stationers' Association Conference of 1930 and a Watcombe fruit bowl for the National Association of Master Bakers, Confectioners and Caterers Conference of 1931 (fig. 49).

The Stationers' Association Conference was held from 2nd to the 4th June 1930 and some 250 delegates attended. Apart from the business sessions their main social activity seems to have been an outing to Plymouth and a dinner dance at the Victoria and Albert Hotel. The Stationery Trade Journal of June 1930 reported '. . . eleven crowded chars-a-bancs started for Plymouth via Totnes'; after lunch at the Royal Hotel in Plymouth hosted by the Mayor, 'the return journey was made over the moors via Princetown and Haytor, and at the latter place everyone sat down with gusto to a delightful Devonshire tea'. The commemoratives made for the Stationers Conference are in the form of a blue pot decorated with a white ink pot and quill pen done in relief and with a white 'icing' inscription: 'The Stationers Association Conference Torquay 1930'. The pots were most probably presented filled with chocolates and were, no doubt, a delightful souvenir of the occasion. The 1957 Stationers Conference at the Grand Atlantic Hotel, Weston-Super-Mare was also commemorated by the Torquay Potteries, but this time in the form of a mottoware butter dish made

by the Watcombe Pottery. The later Conference was attended by fewer delegates, just 200, and the declining popularity of trade conferences after World War II was probably reflected in the inferior commemoratives made of the event!

By comparison with the Stationers' event, the 44th Annual Conference of the National Association of Master Bakers, Confectioners and Caterers was a much grander occasion, probably helped by the fact that the Deputy Mayor of Torquay, Councillor Frank Callard was the son of a former President of the National Association! The headquarters of the week-long Conference was at the Imperial Hotel and the social events included bowls and cricket tournaments, a garden party in the grounds of Torre Abbey (unfortunately rained off!) plus the inevitable excursion over Dartmoor. 'The National Association Review' of June 12th 1931 reported 'There were 1,200 present at the reception and almost as many took part in the whole day trip over Dartmoor to Plymouth' – those Devon lanes must have been very crowded indeed as, in those days 'charas' were small which would have entailed a 'crocodile' of about forty vehicles. In spite of the large number of delegates, the VIP's were, presumably, an exclusive band of people because the commemoratives are very rare; they are in the form of blue fruit bowls eight inches in diameter decorated with a diving Kingfisher with the inscription 'National Association of Master Bakers, Confectioners and Caterers Conference Torquay 1931'.

Sometimes the local Devon Potteries produced their own souvenirs to be given to delegates or guests during visits to the Potteries, presumably as an incentive to purchase other items from the showrooms! Tours of the Potteries were often included in the excursions, and examples of these gifts include scent bottles made for the I.M.E.A. Conference in 1929 and powder bowls for the B.F.M.P. in 1955.

The Incorporated Municipal Electrical Association's Convention was held from 4th to 8th June 1929 at the Pavilion in Torquay. This was one of the few conferences where women played an active role in the business proceedings and Thursday 6th June was set aside as 'Women's Day'. Here Miss M. Partridge, B.Sc., gave what the Torquay Times described as a 'lecturette' entitled 'Women's Work in connection with Rural Electrification in Devon' where she explained that in North Devon women used to say they didn't want 'men tramping through their homes' but 'now that women were employed in installation work quite a different view was taken' and this would mean that many Devonshire villages would be connected to electricity within two years. Miss Partridge acknowledged that some people objected to the overhead cables and poles but, she suggested, 'roses can be grown up them and they can be whitewashed'!! The Torquay Times continued their report 'In the afternoon the ladies attending the Convention visited Longpark Pottery where they spent an interesting time' – presumably also picking up their souvenir scent bottles inscribed 'I.M.E.A. Convention Torquay June 1929' (fig. 49).

The ladies attending the British Federation of Master Printers Congress in Torquay also went on a visit to a local pottery, this time the Royal Watcombe Pottery, where they were given souvenir powder bowls. The bowls are cream coloured with green bands and the lids have been decorated with pink fuschias – altogether a very pretty gift. The commemoration for these is on the base which is inscribed 'B.F.M.P. Congress Torquay 1955' – collectors should note this because without turning the pots upside down it is not obvious they are commemoratives! Because of the inscription, there is no pottery backstamp. The B.F.M.P. had visited Torquay twice before, in 1934 and 1937, although no local pottery commemoratives have been seen for these earlier events.

Many trade organisations commissioned their own commemoratives which would be given, or sold, to delegates and members as a memento of the occasion; these are usually small items such as scent bottles or ashtrays. The Sub-Postmasters Conference in 1937 took place in Plymouth and was hosted by their regional branch, the Western District Council. Conference headquarters was at the Duke of Cornwall Hotel although few of the 200 delegates and visitors could have afforded the tariff of 15/-(75p) a day – most of them would have boarded at cheaper guest houses in the area. The hosts presented all the ladies with scent bottles, made by the Devon Tors Pottery at Bovey Tracey and filled with Devon Violets scent, which were inscribed 'Sub Postmasters Coronation Conference Plymouth 1937' (even though the Conference took place at Easter, some weeks before the Coronation)!

FROM *THE SUB POSTMASTER*

May 1937 Conference Notes
'The little souvenirs given by the District Council to the ladies were valuable and will be highly treasured by the recipients, who will appreciate Devon ware and Devon scent'.

FROM THE *T. & R. BULLETIN* OF THE RADIO SOCIETY OF GREAT BRITAIN, AUGUST 1954

'Made of Devon Pottery and gaily coloured, this attractive ashtray will provide a pleasing souvenir of the Bristol Convention. Members unable to attend the Convention may obtain one of these ashtrays from the Honorary Secretary, Convention Committee, price 3/6d. post free'.

The Radio Society of Great Britain commissioned ashtrays to commemorate their Convention at Bristol from 17th–19th September 1954, although these were offered for sale to all members regardless of whether they attended the Convention or not! The ashtrays were made by the Watcombe Pottery and are decorated with the traditional cottage with the addition of a prominent radio aerial.

Ashtrays were also made as souvenirs for the Building Industries Distributors Conference which took place at the Grand Hotel, Folkestone from 17th to 21st May 1953. The B.I.D. was an organisation devoted to the distribution of building materials during the post-war period when such materials were in short supply, and they worked closely with the Ministry of Works. The special guests in 1953 were a delegation from the Dutch Builders Merchant Federation, with whom they co-operated in post-war reconstruction in Holland. About 300 delegates attended the business sessions and there was plenty of time for the social events which included a banquet as well as golf, bowls, snooker and billiards tournaments –

they must have been an action packed five days! The Watcombe ashtrays are unusual in that they are crown shaped and carry the inscription 'Coronation Conference B.I.D. 1953 Folkestone'.

Another Watcombe commemorative ashtray that has been seen is inscribed simply 'Newquay Conference 1956' – however, as it does not have any other details, *what* it commemorates remains a mystery!

Association meetings, conferences etc. commemorated on Torquay Pottery

1918	R.A.O.B. Pierrot Troupe.
1924	Rotary International Conference, Torquay (Royal Torquay).
1928	R.A.O.B. Ye Pride of Dart Lodge (Royal Torquay).
1928	R.A.O.B. Ye Olde Dick Turpin Lodge, Chudleigh (Devon Tors).
1929	Incorporated Municipal Electrical Association Convention, Torquay (Longpark).
1930	Stationers Association Conference, Torquay (Longpark).
1931	National Association of Master Bakers, Confectioners and Caterers Conference, Torquay (Watcombe).
1931	Dalhousie Lodge Ladies Festival (Watcombe).
1932	Eucharistic Congress, Dublin (Longpark).
1934	British Legion Chudleigh (Devon Tors).
1937	Sub-postmasters Conference, Plymouth (Devon Tors).
1952	George Beech Lodge (Watcombe).

1953	Building Industries Distributors Conference, Folkestone (Watcombe).
1954	Radio Society of Great Britain Convention, Bristol (Watcombe).
1955	British Federation of Master Printers Congress, Torquay (Watcombe).
1956	Newquay Conference (Watcombe).
1957	Stationers Association Conference, Weston-Super-Mare, (Watcombe).
1960	Lodge of Faith Ladies Festival (Babbacombe).

FROM *THE MAGAZINE OF ART 1891*

'The Potteries of Aller Vale' by Cosmo Monkhouse:

'Of all the examples of those 'Home' potteries that I have seen, I like none better than those which carry on the old English traditions – modern descendants of the old 'tygs' and 'posset pots'; and specially, I think, are to be encouraged pieces made for festive occasions, such as births and marriages and birthdays, and decorated with bold flourishes and appropriate mottoes'.

Fig. 44. Commemoratives made for weddings, christenings and anniversaries. Back row, left to right: Longpark teapot decorated with a scandy pattern inscribed 'Mr. and Mrs. Dolbear Silver Wedding April 27th 1924'; Devon Tors teapot covered with gold coloured slip and a white 'icing' inscription 'Congratulations on your Golden Anniversary Year, Here's wishing you Health, Wealth and Lots of Good Cheer 29-10-10 29-10-60; Hart and Moist teapot decorated in slips with coloured scrolls and a horseshoe, inscribed 'A Present to my Sister on the occasion of her Marriage June 4th 1906 from Alfred'. The cups and saucers in front of the teapot were made for the christening of two sons, Frank and Leslie'. On the left at the front: Longpark cup and plate decorated with the crocus pattern, commemorating the christening of 'Terry Edmund Steer, born Dec. 11th 1932'. The two handled mug, made by the Exeter Art Pottery is also a christening present – the reverse is inscribed 'The Little Gem'.

Fig. 45. Personal commemoratives. Left to right: Aller Vale two handled loving cup, nine inches (23 cms.) tall decorated in s'graffito with multi-coloured slips; reverse decorated with an opposing pair of cockerels and a motto 'While I live I'll crow' – probably a family crest; Watcombe vase ten and a half inches (26.5 cms.) tall painted in pigment with a scene of Withycombe Mill, Exmouth, and inscribed on the reverse 'Ada 3.2.09'; Aller Vale three handled tyg with a s'graffito figure of a graduate.

Personal commemoratives

Cosmo Monkhouse writing in the Magazine of Art in 1891 praised the Aller Vale Pottery because it was carrying on the old English traditions of making special individual pieces for festive occasions such as births and marriages and birthdays. Certainly the small potteries were ideally suited for this kind of work and both the potters and customers were encouraged to order special commemoratives. These pieces are still relatively cheap to buy because they commemorate the common man, yet they are usually unique and collectors can enlarge their hobby by researching the background to the pieces. For the general Torquay collector these commemoratives can often be useful in helping to date particular designs as often standard lines were personalised by the addition of a name and date.

Births, marriages and anniversaries were always popular family occasions and a selection of these commemoratives are shown. The amber tyg for Ella Cecilia Jacobs (fig. 44) must have been one of the earliest items made at Exeter Art Pottery and the erratic writing would suggest it was inscribed by the purchaser; its rather a heavy pot to be given to a baby girl! Teapots were a perennial favourite for anniversaries – the globular pot is unusual because an attempt has been made to decorate it in gold suitable for the Golden Wedding it commemorates. An article about Mr.and Mrs.Gilding appeared in the Mid-Devon Times of October

29th 1960 and reported that they were keen travellers and had been to many European countries as well as America; these personal details add 'substance' to what is otherwise a rather plain teapot!

Christmas was a popular time for giving presents of Torquay pottery and often these were personally inscribed (fig. 53) Sometimes the legend was brief such as a Royal Torquay dressing table tray inscribed 'To Lil from Jim Xmas 1929' in other instances there was a personalised motto as on the Longpark mug:

John – if your face wants to smile,
　let it
If it won't, make it.
25th Dec. 1932.

This was in the depths of the Depression perhaps John had nothing to smile about!

Many standard Torquay lines were personalised simply by the addition of a name, or initials, and a date; perhaps these were birthday gifts, or just tokens of a memorable occasion. A large Watcombe vase, decorated with a view of Withycombe Mill, Exmouth, is inscribed on the back 'Ada 3/2/09' – perhaps a favourite spot of Ada's! For local historians, pieces like this have an added significance because Withycombe Mill no longer exists – there had been five mills on the site dating back to the Norman period but after severe flooding in 1960 it was decided to demolish the Mill and the adjoining cottage.

Fig. 46. Personal commemoratives. At the back are three tobacco jars. Left to right: Royal Torquay decorated with cabbage roses and crossed anchors; Crown Dorset, decorated in the Persian pattern, inscribed 'John Russell 1914'; Hart and Moist, decorated in coloured scrolls. The anchor tobacco jar, teapot and two mugs were all made for members of the Bishop family.

Fig. 47. Personal commemoratives. Back row, left to right: Watcombe plate decorated with a mauve iris; dressing table tray, Watcombe, painted in pigment with a view of Cockington Church, Torquay; biscuit barrel decorated with cottages inscribed 'To Kathleen, wishing you a very happy birthday June 25th 1953' made by Sid Udraufski at the Watcombe Pottery. Bottom row: cottageware teapot by Watcombe – the erratic lettering of the inscription indicates it was written by the customer!; pint mug, Watcombe, decorated with a scandy pattern on both sides and incised on the base 'W. Brown to N. Brown'; hatpin holder decorated with a cockerel, made by Longpark and inscribed 'V.E.M. 1910' Devon Tors mug decorated with a cottage, inscribed 'C.H.Staddon 80 today' – he was a cousin of 'Nocky' (Enoch) Staddon, director of the Royal Torquay Pottery; cup and saucer made by Royal Torquay 'To Ethel from Harry'.

Occasionally collectors may be lucky enough to come across truly individual pieces, such as the Aller Vale three-handled vase with a s'graffito drawing of a graduate (fig. 45). From the stance, this must have been copied from a photograph; it is, unfortunately, not named or dated but, on stylistic grounds, must have been made about 1890. Another Aller Vale mug is inscribed 'Gertie 27th Jany 1896' on one side, and on the reverse it is decorated with an opposing pair of heraldic cockerels surrounding a small flower head, beneath which is the motto 'While I live I'll crow' – surely a family crest and motto.

FROM *THE POTTERY GAZETTE*

March 1st 1907 – Article on the Watcombe Pottery.
'The Company are also applying Devonshire scenes to numerous useful and ornamental pieces. These are nicely executed in colours on shaded grounds'.

Fig. 48. Commemoratives made for children. These are examples of typical Torquay mottowares with personalised inscriptions.

Some of the inscriptions seen on personalised commemoratives.

Edna
From Leslie and Elsie
Xmas 1930
(Cup and saucer).

To Mrs. Horwill
From Mr. and Mrs. Prescott
1919
(Royal Torquay plant holder).

V.E.M. 1910
I'll take care of the pins.
(Longpark hatpin holder).

A happy birthday
To Mother
With love from Doris 1916
(Cup and saucer).

A present to my sister on the
occasion of her marriage
June 4th 1906
From Alfred

To Ethel and Fred
Xmas 1934
From Lily
(Watcombe faience vase decorated
with a beach scene).

Mr. and Mrs. A. G. Gilding
Congratulations on your Golden
Anniversary Year
Here's wishing you health, wealth
and a lot of good cheer.
29.10.10–29.10.60.

Mr. and Mrs. Dolbear
Silver Wedding April 27th 1924.
May you live as long as you want
And never want as long as you live

Gertrude Lucy Kent
Given to her on her 8th birthday
April 15th 1907
(Cup and saucer).

With best wishes to my wife
From George
Xmas 1919
(Royal Torquay biscuit barrel).

This life is but a little span
Let's all be friends just while we can

The milk of human kindness
Is often lost through blindness

A kindly word will alway be
As sweet as sugar in the tea

The above three Mottoes on teapot,
milk jug and sugar bowl inscribed:
'W. H. Groom with best wishes from
B. P. and G. P.'

Denis Sawtrey Christmas 1932
The slump may depress you and fill
    you with gloom
Forget it and think what you'll do in
    the boom.

FROM *THE POTTERY GAZETTE*

September 1st 1913 – Article on Royal Aller Vale and Watcombe Art Potteries.
'The proprietors of the two potteries in question are always pleased to show visitors round their works, and no one spending a holiday in the vicinity should fail to take advantage of the offer, for the visit cannot fail to prove well worth the time'.

Commemoratives for masonic and similar clubs

Many Clubs and Associations commissioned their own commemoratives to be given to officers or members for special events such as banquets. Those given to officers are often quite splendid and are sometimes unique. Examples of these are the Watcombe pieces made for the Dalhousie Masonic Lodge Ladies Festival in 1931 (fig. 52). Two versions have been seen for this event – a vase twelve inches tall decorated with a diving Kingfisher on a blue ground, and a biscuit barrel decorated with geometric shapes of colour in Art Deco style. Only one biscuit barrel has been seen, although there are at least two of the vases: all have the same inscription 'Dalhousie Lodge No. 860 Ladies Festival 1931'; this Lodge is at Freemasons Hall, Great Queen Street, London. These were most likely gifts for the wives of Lodge officials on Ladies Night as it is unlikely that such elaborate (and expensive) items would have been given to all the ladies.

Another gift for the wives of committee members was the Torquay Pottery bowls made to commemorate the Rotary International Conference held in Torquay in 1924. This was a prestigious event for the Torquay Rotary Club as they had been founded only two years previously and they were, no doubt, anxious to create a good impression! The bowls were designed by Mr. White, a lecturer at Torquay Art College and they were intended to hold chocolates; they were presented to the ladies whilst the men were given fountain pens! The bowls are decorated with the crest of the Rotary Club in white, and are inscribed 'Service not Self 1924 Torquay Conference' – the motto is the Rotary Club's original motto, which was changed at the 1924 Conference. The bowls were presumably highly regarded because a similar design was used by Longpark for their Stationers Conference commemorative in 1930.

Several branches of the Royal Antedeluvian Order of Buffaloes are known to have commissioned small mugs which are believed to have been given to the children of members at Christmas. Possibly some may have been presented to recipients of the Christmas Dinners organised by some branches. Those that have been seen include a Royal Torquay mug decorated with applied buffalo horns inscribed 'Present from Ye Pride of Dart Lodge 1928', and a Devon Tors mug decorated with a floral branch and the inscription 'Xmas 1928 Ye Olde Dick Turpin Lodge Chudleigh R.A.O.B.' (fig. 52).

Some associations produced ashtrays which were given out as souvenirs to members at a particular event. One of these is a Watcombe cottageware ashtray which is inscribed 'Hearty fraternal greetings from W. Bro. W. T. Burden Wo. Master 1952 George Beech Lodge No. 2897 Consecrated 12 Apl. 1902' – presumably made to commemorate the Golden Jubilee of the Lodge. A very late example is the blue ashtray, made by the Babbacombe Pottery with the simple 'icing' inscription 'Souvenir of the Lodge of Faith Ladies Festival 6th Feb. 1960 H.S.O.'

THE 'SALLY WILLIAMS' PIN TRAY

Sometimes collectors come across commemorative wares with intriguing inscriptions such as the Sally Williams pin tray (or ashtray) pictured in fig. 50. Researching these inscriptions can provide a fascinating and rewarding extension to the hobby of collecting.

At least three different versions of the tray have been seen and three copies of one version are known to exist. Sally Williams died in 1836 yet the trays date from the time of the Great War; why was this lady commemorated so many years after her death?

Since the tray has a place name, Christchurch, this was the obvious town to begin investigations. Christchurch Priory proved informative because there is a board high on the wall which gives an extract from the will of Sally Williams of Poole, Dorset, and her charity bequest:

'I do also give and bequeath to the vicar and churchwardens for the time being of the parish of Christchurch in the County of Southampton one hundred pounds to be by them placed in some of the government funds of this Kingdom in the name of the late Sally Mitchell for ever there to remain and the annual interest and dividends therefore arising annually on the 29th day of December in every year to pay unto and divide between 5 poor widows and 5 poor maiden women residing in the parish of Christchurch such as they shall think most needing of assistance.'

This established that Sally Williams left a bequest in the name of Sally Mitchell, whose relationship to Sally Williams is not made clear. The records at Christchurch indicate that Sally Williams was buried in the churchyard but the headstones are so worn that it is impossible to find which one is hers.

The next source of information was

Fig. 49. Items to commemorate Conferences. Top row, left to right: powder bowl decorated on the lid with pink fuschias, made by Watcombe and inscribed on the base 'B.F.M.P. Congress Torquay 1955'; ashtray moulded in the shape of a crown for the British Industries Distributors Coronation Conference 1953; round ashtray decorated with a cottage sporting a radio aerial inscribed 'R.S.G.B. Convention Bristol Sept. 1954' square ashtray inscribed 'Newquay Conference 1956' – all three ashtrays by Watcombe. Bottom row: two scent bottles, decorated with Kingfishers and inscribed 'I.M.E.A. Convention Torquay 1929 – made by Longpark; Devon Tors scent bottles for the 'Sub-Postmasters Coronation Conference 1937'; Watcombe covered butter dish for the Stationers Conference, Weston Super Mare 1937; Watcombe bowl decorated with a Kingfisher and inscribed around the rim 'National Association of Master Bakers, Confectioners and Caterers Conference Torquay 1931'; Longpark chocolate bowl for the Stationers Association Conference, Torquay 1930.

the will itself, lodged in the Public Record Office in London. Sally Williams wrote her last will on 5th December 1831 when she was 74 years of age. In addition to the charity, she left over £1,300 in bequests to 23 specified people, ranging from £5 to her friend Mrs.Martha Bartlett of Weymouth, up to £200 to her cousin, Mrs.Martha Porter of Naples. From the will it can be assumed that Sally Williams was a widow because she names 'two nieces by marriage' yet her husband was not mentioned so presumably he was already dead. No children were mentioned either so this must surely mean there were none, or at least none surviving, nor any grandchildren.

Sally Williams seems to have been a women with strong views about certain matters. For instance, the residue of her will was left to her cousin, William Mitchell, in trust for his children on his death, with the condition 'provided they are not catholics'! Sally's father's gold watch and silver tankard and silver teapot were bequeathed to her cousin's son, William, 'never to be sold unless for bread'. Reading 'between the lines' there seem to be some intriguing innuendos too; for instance £250 was left to her cousin, Richard

Fig. 50. Ashtray/pintray commemorating the Sally Williams Charity, made by Watcombe.

Bursoy of Newfoundland and his children 'lawfully begotten'; was he, perhaps, a man prone to sow his wild oats?!

In spite of the will being long and detailed, it does not say who 'the late Sally Mitchell' was, in whose name the charity was lodged. Since Sally Williams had a cousin with the surname, the possibility arises that Sally Mitchell was her mother. There is also no indication as to why Sally Williams 'died of grief' as the inscription on the trays record. Perhaps it was engraved on her tombstone, which was probably readable seventy years ago, or maybe it was just a 'turn of phrase' not meant to be an accurate statement.

All this research provides an interesting background to the Sally Williams story but it does not explain why the trays were made. Christchurch Priory still administers the charity but the income from the £100 investment is very modest today; one logical answer could be that the trays were given to 'five poor widows and 5 poor maiden women' as a reminder of their rich, but somewhat eccentric, benefactor.

Sporting commemoratives

South Devon was a popular area for sporting tours, as the participants could combine their sports with a holiday, and some of these visits were recorded by commemoratives. In some cases the visiting teams returned on several occasions so collectors may be lucky enough to acquire a series of these souvenirs.

One of the earliest of these sports commemoratives was made for the New Zealand Rugby Tour in 1905. The All Blacks arrived in London in September 1905 with a week to spare and asked to be recommended a town where they could train in peace and quiet – Newton Abbot was chosen and the tourists enjoyed their stay so much that they returned in 1924 and 1935! Newton Abbot was initially taken by surprise and there were no official engagements, although the locals were most hospitable! The players practised every morning and during the afternoons they walked or cycled around the district, perhaps even visiting the local potteries as the commemoratives would suggest. The Aller Vale Pottery produced a beaker to commemorate the occasion, it is most unusual in that it portrays the heads of the King and Queen surrounded by patriotic flowers, as on the 1902 Coronation commemoratives. On the reverse is a fern leaf in relief with 'N.Z.' in slip and the date 1905; underneath is the s'graffito inscription 'A souvenir of the Royal Aller Vale and Watcombe Potteries, Newton Abbot, Devon'. Inside the rim are the words 'Kia Ora' in cream slip. The beakers were also inscribed with the names of individual players.

When the New Zealanders returned to Newton Abbot in 1924 the town was well prepared. A reception committee had organised a series of social events including a Ball at the

Globe Hotel (their headquarters), an afternoon at the races and a visit to the Watcombe Potteries – this was probably inevitable since Mr. Wallace Hexter, one of the directors of the Watcombe Pottery, was on the organising committee! The Pottery produced large waisted mugs, five and three quarters inches tall, decorated with the scandy pattern and the inscription 'Souvenir of the visit of the New Zealand Football Team to Newton Abbot Devon 1924–25 Kia Ora'; the mugs are individually named and were given to all the players and committee members.

The 1935 tour was also a highly organised affair although there were fewer social events as it was a shorter visit. The Watcombe commemoratives were in the style of the 1924 mugs but were decorated with fern leaves painted in pigment. The large mugs were named for players and committee members but small unnamed versions were also made – these were possibly given as souvenirs to all those attending the Reception Banquet.

The Sun Life Cricket Team had an annual tour to Torquay and they, like the All Blacks, commemorated the event with souvenir mugs. The second tour, in 1935, was the first to be commemorated with a pint mug decorated with a cockerel and made by the Longpark Pottery. In 1936 the Sun team went to Devon Tors for a mug decorated with Uncle Tom Cobley. Both the cockerel and Uncle Tom Cobley were standard decorations, but in 1937 and 1938 special designs were used featuring the cricket pavilions of Newton Abbot and Exmouth – those are finely painted in slips and were all done by the same girl at Devon Tors. After World War II the quality of the mugs declined, partly due to wartime re-

FROM THE *MID DEVON ADVERTISER*

September 13th 1924.
The members of the All Black Team, now nearing the end of their sojourn in Newton Abbot, express themselves as delighted with the hearty welcome they have received, and with the arrangements made for their training and their amusement by the Local Reception Committee... On Saturday morning they paid a visit to the Watcombe Potteries, and in the afternoon again journeyed to Torquay to witness the game in which Camborne were engaged...

strictions but also due to rising costs. The 1948 mug was made by Watcombe and was simply a green glaze over cream slip. After that the team went to the newly opened Babbacombe Pottery, although a few of the later items were made at Devon Tors again, then Sandygate – by this time the mugs were moulded and slip cast, no longer the hand thrown pieces using local clays! About fifteen or sixteen mugs were made for each tour and they were inscribed 'Sun of Canada C.C. South Devon Tour' plus the year and the name of the team member. These are obviously very rare, but it is possible that other teams ordered similar items which have not yet come to light!

A very personal sporting commemorative was made at Longpark Pottery for H. Snape, Captain of the Torquay Cricket Club second eleven 1947–53; this is in the form of an ashtray and was signed on the back 'Reg Stuckey' – he was one of the best throwers and worked for several of the Torquay Potteries.

Fig. 51. Sporting Commemoratives. Left to right: two Devon Tors pint mugs both made for the Sun of Canada Cricket tours, the one on the left being decorated with Exmouth cricket pavilion for the 1938 tour, and on the right, mug decorated with Uncle Tom Cobley for the 1936 tour; yellow ashtray made by Longpark for 'H. Snape, Torquay Cricket Club 2nd XI, Captain 1947–53'; two mugs and beaker all made to commemorate the All Blacks Tours – the beaker is for the 1905 tour, large waisted mug for the 1924/5 tour and the small waisted beaker for the 1935–36 tour. Souvenir programme for the 1935–36 tour.

SUN OF CANADA Cricket Tours – mugs made:

1934 First tour of Devon – no mugs made.

1935 Longpark mug decorated with a cockerel.

1936 Devon Tors mug decorated with Uncle Tom Cobley.

1937 Devon Tors mug decorated with Newton Abbot cricket ground.

1938 Devon Tors mug decorated with Exmouth Cricket Club pavilion.

1939–47 No Tours.

1948 Watcombe mug with inscription only under a green glaze.

1949–52 Babbacombe mug to commemorate 4 years decorated with a cream maple leaf on dark blue ground.

1953 Babbacombe mug decorated with blue maple leaf on yellow ground.

1954 Babbacombe mug decorated with a cream maple leaf on blue band encircling a yellow mug.

1955 Babbacombe mug decorated with cricket stumps on a blue ground.

1956	Devon Tors mug decorated with a maple leaf on a green ground.	1960	White moulded mug with maple leaf – made in Paignton, pottery not known.
1957	Devon Tors mug decorated with a yellow maple leaf on a bright blue ground.	1961	Round Devon Tors ashtray, yellow with bright blue interior.
1958	As 1957, slightly darker blue.	1962	Similar to 1961 but triangular shaped.
1959	Sandygate moulded mug decorated with a white maple leaf on a sage green/grey mug.	1970	Grey thrown mug with tour results – made at the Wellhouse Pottery, Brixham.

Fig. 52. Masonic Associations and similar Clubs. Back row: Watcombe biscuit barrel and Kingfisher vase twelve inches (30.5 cms.) tall both inscribed 'Dalhousie Lodge, No. 860, Ladies Festival 1931'; Royal Torquay chocolate bowl for the Rotary International Conference 1924. Bottom row: Babba-combe ashtray inscribed 'Souvenir of Lodge of Faith Ladies Festival 6th Feb. 1960 HSO'; round Watcombe ashtray for George Beech Lodge 1902–1952; Devon Tors mug for the RAOB, Chudleigh 1928; RAOB mug with applied buffalo horns, made by Royal Torquay, and inscribed 'Present from Ye Pride of Dart Lodge 1928'.

ADVERTISING WARES

lthough aggressive and gim-
micky advertising is very
much a modern phenomenon,
craftsmen have always needed to
advertise their trades in order to get
customers. In the Middle Ages commercial life was very localised so arti-
sans had a captive market, but during
the religious persecution in Europe
following the Reformation thousands
of Protestant Flemings came to Britain
and brought their ideas and skills
with them. This was particularly evi-
dent in potting where the continental
styles of slip trailing and warm yellow
lead glazes began to influence British
potters. By the middle of the 17th century a new business was developing
whereby pedlars would travel around
the countryside with pots for sale.
This brought competition to local potteries and a more discerning customer! Thus, the better potters were
anxious to advertise their wares and
they began to mark their pots with
their place of origin e.g. Thomas Toft
chargers which often incorporate his
name into the decoration. With the
onset of the Industrial Revolution this
process accelerated – a punchbowl
made by the Chailey Pottery was decorated with a motto followed by 'Thos.
Alcorn Chailey South Common Potteries Sussex 1792'. By the mid-nineteenth
century it was becoming common for
pots to be marked with the name of a
retailer either in addition to, or instead
of, the manufacturer; these marks were
increasingly relegated to the base of the
pot, rather than as part of the
decoration.

The practice of marking goods with
their place of manufacture or retail
was a very modest form of advertising, but with the growth of competition advertising techniques became
more forceful. One of the 'fathers' of
this new profession of advertising
was Thomas Barrett, a director of A. &
F. Pears Soap Company and this was
to bring him into contact with the Torquay Potteries. In 1878 Barrett attended the Paris Exhibition and was
impressed by a plaster-of-Paris model
he saw there depicting an old woman
washing a boy; this, he believed,
could be the basis of an advertising
campaign for Pears Soap, so he
bought the model for 100 guineas.
The model was sculpted by an impov-
erished Italian sculptor called Giovanni Focardi, who had been staying
in an attic room at Preston in Lancash-
ire. Whilst there, he sketched his
landlady washing her grandson in the
back yard and this formed the basis of
his model known as 'You Dirty Boy'.
Barrett arranged for the model to be
sculpted in marble for Pears' London
office and in terracotta as advertisements for the shops that sold the
soap. Millions of handbills showing
You Dirty Boy were distributed
worldwide, and small novelty alabaster models were made as a promotional gimmick.

The terracotta figures of 'You Dirty
Boy' were made by both the Watcombe Pottery and the Torquay Terracotta Company using the same
moulds (Inside Front Cover). They
are 26 inches tall and the detailing is
superb, particularly on the old
woman's face and the boy's where
even his tears are visible! These figure
groups were intended for display in
alcoves etc. outside shops and as a
result many have weathered badly; in
any case the boy's arms are especially
vulnerable to knocks and many
examples are broken or damaged.
Hundreds of those figures must have

been made as they were used to advertise Pears Soap from 1878 until about the time of World War 1. Snowden Ward, writing in the Art Journal in 1900 about the Watcombe Pottery, commented:

'The terracotta side is still continued: the Lascoon group, the Venus de Milo, the Discobolus and many another Art School inspiration is produced alongside the busts of modern statesmen and musical composers, but their sale sinks into insignificance compared with the demand for certain advertising statuettes, and even these do not find occupation for the extensive buildings made for them.'

The Dirty Boy figures are usually just plain terracotta although a painted example has been seen, possibly decorated by a diligent shopkeeper! Both the advertising handbills and the small alabaster models have 'Pears' written on the washing bowl, but this is missing from the terracotta group – why this is so remains a mystery!

The Pears advertising group showed the artistic skills of the potters

FROM *THE* POTTERY GAZETTE

September 1st 1913.
'Not only is the Watcombe factory entailed in the manufacture of readily saleable souvenirs, but also in the production of vases of classical forms with embellishments not merely the result of the brush, but of the mould. It produces some very effectively modelled statuettes and groups, and the pair known as 'You dirty boy' manufactured for A. & F. Pears Ltd. of soap fame, is an illustration of the resources of their modellers'.

at their very best, however the majority of subsequent advertising pieces were much more mundane and their interest to collectors comes with their rarity and the product they advertise rather than artistic merit! Devon was known as the 'land of cream and cider' so it was perhaps natural that these should figure amongst the early advertising pottery.

'The land of cream and cider'

One of the first dairies to promote their wares in Torquay pottery was not local at all but a London Company, the West London Dairy which had a dozen or so branches stretching from Kilburn to Chiswick and as far east as Greenwich. They began as the West London Dairy Society in the mid 1880's, changing the 'Society' to 'Company' in 1890; they eventually went out of business around the time of the Great War. The jug and small churns (fig. 55) were made as promotional items in the early 1900s by the Aller Vale Pottery and must be some of their earliest advertising wares.

Some twenty years later, in the 1920s the Longpark Pottery produced advertising teapots for J. W. Humphrey's & Sons whose dairy operated from 1 Station Road, Chadwell Heath, Esssex, from c.1919 to 1930, when it was bought out by Unigate. The teapots are decorated with the scandy pattern and carry the message 'A small piece of Devonshire Ware wishing our friends a Happy New Year' – unfortunately they do not state *which* New Year was being celebrated, although possibly this was so they could be used the following year if any were left over!

The Priory Farm Dairy at Taunton also commissioned a dual purpose advertising product but theirs was a cream bowl to commemorate the Coronation of King George V1 in 1937. The bowl was made by the Watcombe Pottery and was one of their standard cottageware lines, the gabled cottage being of the type favoured by Bill Critchlow. The Priory Farm Dairy was established in 1896 and at the time of the Coronation was in the ownership of Walter John Howe; it continued as a dairy until 1971 and the premises are now used by a company trading in Christmas decorations and novelties.

The West Country was famous for its apple orchards and there were many small companies turning these apples into cider, or 'cyder' as it was more commonly known. The benefits of drinking cider were enormous – an advertisement in the Devon Evening Express in 1901 claimed that cider was 'an infallible counteractant for Gout, Rheumatism, Gravel, Stone, Uric Acid and Impaired Sight', the last being somewhat dubious since more people's sight was probably impaired by drinking too much 'scrumpy' than were ever cured by it!!.

Fig. 54 shows a variety of Torquay Pottery items made to advertise cider

Fig. 53. Personal commemoratives. All made as Christmas gifts. The cups and saucers on the top shelf were made by Watcombe, teapot, milk jug and sugar bowl by Longpark. Bottom row, left to right: Watcombe vase painted underglaze with a scene of Babbacombe beach; Royal Torquay biscuit barrel decorated with ships in a rosy sunset scene; dressing table tray by Royal Torquay with a seagull on a rock on dark green ground – this is unusual because the normal ground colour for this standard decoration was blue; blue Longpark mug with 'icing inscription'; Royal Torquay hanging plant pot which seems to have been converted from a biscuit barrel! In front, a match holder/ashtray inscribed: 'The slump may depress you and fill you with gloom Forget it and think what you'll do in the boom. It is dated 1932, the depths of the Depression!

Fig. 54. Selection of items advertising Cider companies. Top shelf: Longpark jug decorated with an apple advertising 'Hunts Cider'; Devon Tors jug decorated with a view of Dunsford village inscribed 'Meadhay Cider Company'; Watcombe waisted mug decorated with an apple, inscribed on the reverse 'Symons Cider, Totnes Devon, Ratcliffe London'; Bottom row: Ginger shaker made by Watcombe for the Taunton Cider Company; Henley's Cyder jug and mug, both by Longpark; Watcombe cider flagon inscribed 'Blue Ball Inn near Lynmouth'. The Henley's advertisement is from a trade directory of 1902.

companies. Of these, the most well-known is probably Henley's Cider, whose advertisements claimed they were established in 1791; by the mid 1870s they had offices in London and were exporting widely. Their advertising wares were typically jugs and mugs, made by the Longpark Pottery, and decorated with their standard cockerel pattern; they date from the Edwardian period and were probably made until the 1920s. Henley's was taken over in 1933 by Whiteways and are now part of the Showerings Group.

A more unusual cider mug is that made by the Watcombe Pottery for Symons which is decorated with apples. John Symons established his business at Totnes c.1873 and eventually owned a London depot at Ratcliff E.14, as shown on the mug. The Company also made a non-alcoholic cider, known as Sydrina, although no advertising mugs have been seen with this name. Symons appear to have gone out of business during World War II, a fate that befell many businesses including Meadhay Ltd, fruit farmers and cider makers of Christow

67

Fig. 55. Advertising dairy products. On the left: jug and two churns advertising West London Dairy Company Ltd., made by Aller Vale to hold cream; Longpark teapot decorated with a scandy pattern to advertise 'J. W. Humphrey's & Son, Dairy specialist, Chadwell Heath'; Watcombe cream bowl decorated with a cottage, made as a souvenir of the 'Coronation, May 1937' – inscribed on the base 'Priory Farm Dairy, Taunton'.

near Dunsford, who commissioned an advertising mug from the Devon Tors Pottery at nearby Bovey Tracey. Unlike Henleys and Symons, Meadhay's had a very short life, as they only began production in the late 1930s.

Many established cider drinkers liked to add spice to their favourite tipple by sprinkling ginger on the top. The Taunton Cider Company commissioned special ginger shakers from the Watcombe Pottery which carried the invitation 'How 'bout a bit O GINGER in thee's CIDUR' The shakers are 4 inches tall and were made with either an amber or a blue glaze: they were produced as a promotional item about 1930 and were distributed to publicans within the Taunton Cider distribution area (a ra-

dius of about seventy miles from Taunton). The Company still practices the ancient pagan custom of wassailing the apple orchards every January; this necessitates the staff going to the orchards with bowls of mulled cider to sprinkle in and around the apple trees. The party then frighten away bad spirits by banging pans and even firing shotguns into the branches; any cider that is left over is quaffed, followed by a good deal of dancing and merry making. The purpose of wassailing is to ensure a good apple crop, and hence good cider, at the next harvest – judging by the success of the Taunton Cider Company, it appears to work!.

Many tourists who got a taste for cider whilst in the West Country, liked to take some back for their

68

friends to try. The Blue Ball Inn near Lynmouth commissioned small cider flagons from the Watcombe Pottery to be filled with their own vintage cider. These provided a useful souvenir which also advertised the Inn.

Pub mugs

Mugs, or tankards, depicting particular pubs became very popular during the 1930s and seem to have been a particular speciality of the Devon Tors Pottery at Bovey Tracey. The slip painted decorations are often beautifully done, but it is questionable whether they are strictly advertising wares. Many old pubs such as the Sloop Inn at St. Ives or the Three Pilchards Inn at Polperro were tourist attractions and no doubt some of these mugs would have been sold in souvenir shops alongside pottery decorated with local views. However, some mugs were sold in pubs and were, as such, advertising wares. An example of this is the mug for the Old Commercial Inn at Bishopsteignton, Devon, which is inscribed:

North, South
   East, or West
Bill Mole's
   is the best.

Bill Mole took over as landlord of the Old Commercial Inn in the mid 1920s and was said to be the youngest landlord in the West Country. He played rugby for Devon and was a member of the team that played the All Blacks during their tour of 1924. The pint mugs were sold at the pub for 2/6d. each (twelve and a half pence), and probably date from the late 1930s or 1940s. Bill Mole died at the end of 1955 and was succeeded by the present landlady – testimony indeed that it is a popular pub! The name was changed by the brewers in the late 1960s to the 'Bishop John de Grandisson', a bishop of Exeter whose palace was at Bishopsteignton, in order to give the pub a more 'upmarket' appeal!! A selection of pub mugs is shown in fig. 58, and it is up to collectors to decide if they are 'advertising' wares or not! Whatever the decision, they certainly make an attractive and colourful display – collectors might also like to look for mugs made by different potteries for the same pub, such as the Sloop Inn at St. Ives made by Devon Tors and Dartmouth, or the three versions of the Foxhunter Inn at Westdown near Ilfracombe made by Devon Tors, Dartmouth and the Brannam Pottery at Barnstaple.

Fig. 56 and Fig. 57. 'Henley's Devonshire Cyder' mug by Longpark; Symons cyder mug by Watcombe.

Miscellaneous

Sometimes collectors come across items which were made to publicise various organisations rather than to advertise a commercial enterprise, although they share a similar objective – to raise funds or attract membership! Some are shown in fig. 59.

The Longpark Pottery produced plates, six inches in diameter, with a plain blue band around the rim and an inscription in the middle 'St. Marychurch and Babbacombe Y.M.C.A.' The Young Men's Christian Association and its sister organisation the Young Women's Christian Association, were popular organisations during the first half of the twentieth century for their dedication to the moral and physical welfare of the young. They provided hostels, clubs and activities, with emphasis on working class young people who lived away from home. The Royal Family took a particular interest in the Y.M.C.A. and the Y.W.C.A., and in 1936 Princess Helena Victoria, granddaughter of Queen Victoria, visited the Y.M.C.A. in Torquay, Paignton and St. Marychurch where she received purses for their charity work. The Longpark plates, although earlier in date, were probably made for fund raising.

Another fund raising and publicity item was the Watcombe collecting box made for the R.S.P.C.A. (Royal Society for the Prevention of Cruelty to Animals); it is made of white clay and is in the form of a blue glazed box supporting a model of a pair of horses, glazed in brown, overall

Fig. 58. Selection of pub mugs and Devon Tors plate advertising The Copper Kettle at St. Ives, Cornwall. Mugs, left to right: Devon Tors mugs for the Commercial Inn at Bishopsteignton; Dartmouth mug for the Sloop Inn, St. Ives; 'Cheerio' mug by Devon Tors, inscribed on the reverse 'From the Three Pilchards Inn Polperro'; three mugs all advertising the Foxhunters Inn, Westdown near Ilfracombe made by Brannam, Devon Tors and Dartmouth.

Fig. 59. Selection of items advertising products and organisations. On the left, matchstriker and ashtray to advertise L.O.R. Tweddle & Co., capsule makers; across back: Watcombe collecting box made to raise money for the R.S.P.C.A.'s Fund for Sick and Wounded Horses in World War I; Hart and Moist bottle flask advertising Purnell's bottled sunshine which was a brand of coal; model of a boat made by Watcombe to advertise the Berthon Boat Company at Romsey. Middle row: St. Marychurch and Babbacombe Y.M.C.A. plate made by Longpark; Wood Fibre Wallboard Company ashtray, West-brick ashtray decorated with white polka dots on a blue ground, and Vespa Club ashtray all made by Watcombe.

height five inches. The whole box should fit onto a wooden collecting box in aid of the R.S.P.C.A. Fund for Sick and Wounded Horses, which was set up at the start of World War I. The British are known as a nation of animal lovers, so this fund would have had particular appeal. The R.S.P.C.A. placed an advertisement in the Torquay Times of January 29th 1915 which posed a very emotional question: 'War-torn, wounded, weary! What are you doing for us?' With the rapid advances in military technology it is perhaps difficult to appreciate the importance of horses

during the Great War; the advertisement informed its readers that the R.S.P.C.A. had provided 'a Veterinary Hospital to accommodate 1,000 Horses' as well as training for 200 men to enlist in the British Army Veterinary Corps. 'Many letters of thanks from officers at the front and at home have been received showing the work of the R.S.P.C.A. FUND FOR SICK AND WOUNDED HORSES to be absolutely essential'. – and the advertisement concluded 'WILL YOU HELP IT TO CARRY ON?' Who could refuse this worthy cause?! The Watcombe collecting boxes are very rare

71

because most would have either been returned to the R.S.P.C.A., or disposed of, when the War was over.

An equally rare item, but one made for happier occasions is the little model of an iron made by the Torquay Pottery publicising Dymchurch Holiday Camp (fig. 60). The Camp, known as Beach Holiday Centre, opened in 1933 at Dymchurch, near Folkestone in Kent; and by the time it closed in 1968 some 250,000 holidaymakers had passed through its doors. The irons, which have a recess in the top to be used as ashtrays, have been seen in two versions – one decorated with a scandy pattern on a cream ground has the motto 'The world is full of rubs', and the other shows a seagull perched on a rock on a bright blue background. This is inscribed 'The weakest goes to the wall'. Both versions were made in the 1930s.

One of the last publicity items to be made at the Watcombe Pottery must be the triangular shaped ashtray inscribed 'Vespa Club Torquay and Newton'; it is decorated in shades of mustard, pink and blue with brown painted lettering on a cream ground – the colours used by the Pottery for their range of 'contemporary wares' introduced in the late 1950s. Vespas were what a Mid-Devon Times reporter described as 'the little things that race around the corner when you're least expecting them' in an article published on 23rd January 1960

– little scooters, invented by the Italians, which became a craze in Britain in the 1950s. The Torbay and Newton Vespa Club was formed in 1956 by just nine proud owners, but their numbers escalated rapidly so that by 1960 150 members and guests attended their Annual Dinner. The Club was registered with the Vespa Club of Britain as Number 74 and its badge showed Newton's clock tower flanked by palm trees of Torquay. Although the Club was disbanded in the 1970s the former members still hold occasional re-unions; the ex-committee members believe that they were shown samples of the ashtrays with a view to commissioning some as souvenirs but they rejected the idea. This would seem to be substantiated because the ashtrays are inscribed 'Torquay and Newton' whereas the Club was the 'Torbay and Newton' branch!

Fig. 61. Dark brown bottle flask, decorated on the obverse with a fish amongst weeds. Made by Hart and Moist to advertise 'Purnell's bottled sunshine' which was a brand of coal. Height of flask: seven and a half inches (19 cms.).

Fig. 60. Miniature irons made by Royal Torquay to advertise 'Dymchurch Holiday Camp' – they were intended for use as ashtrays.

For advertising products

The Torquay Potteries were commissioned to make individual pieces to advertise particular products – indeed, the terracotta figure group for Pears Soap comes into this category, although the artistic quality of this piece puts it in a class of its own! The majority of other wares are much more ordinary and range from adaptations of the potteries' standard lines to specially commissioned designs.

The Western Counties Company of Exeter ordered a seemingly endless variety of ashtrays to advertise their bricks. These ranged from the standard cream and s'graffito mottowares of the 1920s and 30s to the blue and white polka dot pattern favoured in the 1950s; all are inscribed 'West Brick – Best Brick'. Judging by the ease by which collectors can find these ashtrays, they must have been distributed to virtually all the building contractors and merchants in the West Country!

In some instances, a standard pattern might be modified slightly to suit the customers' product; an example of this is the ashtray made for the Wood Fibre Wallboard Company where a standard cottageware design has a trail of smoke issuing from the chimney which divides the advertising maxims 'Warm in Winter. Cool in Summer'.

Ashtrays figure widely in advertising products made during an era when smoking was a fashionable social habit. Two versions of specially designed ashtrays were made by Watcombe for L. O. R. Tweddle & Co. Ltd. capsule makers of 297 Goswell Road, London E.C.1. (fig. 59). This company made metal caps to go on bottles etc. and they were in business from 1925 to 1937/38. The earlier design is a large flat ashtray with a painting of a cap in the tray, with a motto around the rim – 'Pessimism never paid a dividend' – probably made during the time of the Depression! The second design is more elaborate and is in the form of a combination matchholder, striker and ashtray. The matchholder is modelled as a cap, painted in burgundy with line drawings of patriotic plants; roses, thistles and shamrocks. Tweddle and Co. presumably judged their customers to be well-educated because the rim is inscribed with a latin motto 'Facile princeps' (an easy first).

One advertising piece that could be classified as 'art pottery' is a bottle flask, made by the Exeter Art Pottery, decorated in slips with a fish amongst reeds on a dark brown ground (fig. 61) the reverse has 'SUNSHINE' piped diagonally across the bottle. The base of the pot is impressed 'Purnell's bottled sunshine Reg. No. 423051'. This must rank as one of the most unusual advertising pieces ever produced because 'Purnell's bottled Sunshine' was a brand of coal! T. B. Purnell & Sons began business in the early 1880s as coal and coke merchants, and continued until 1971. In the 1890s, they also became agents for the Union Castle Mail Steamship Co. Ltd., and the Employers Liability Assurance Corporation Ltd., which seems a most unusual combination of business interests! Purnell's advertised their coal extensively in the local press, and in the 'Western Times' of April 2nd 1901, they claimed 'Unsolicited Testimonials are continually being received for the excellence of our Bottled Sunshine, the best coal in the Kingdom'. A contemporary photograph of Purnell's offices at 263 High Street, Exeter, shows two bottle flasks inscribed 'Sunshine' painted on the walls above the entrance, and what looks like two advertising flasks in the window, alongside various

Fig. 62. Mineral Water advertisements. On the left, five items advertising 'Camwal Table Waters'; matchstriker and inkwell for the Salutaris Water Co. and matchstriker for 'Biscombe's Mineral Waters'. All made by the Watcombe Pottery.

other bottles; did these perhaps contain aids to firelighting (e.g. paraffin) or even grate blackening solutions? Whatever the purpose of the bottle flasks, though, they are rare and decorative advertising items.

An unusual novelty advertising piece must be the model of the Berthon boat nine inches long, made by the Watcombe Pottery for the Berthon Boat Company of Romsey and Lymington. The Berthon boat was designed by the Reverend Edward Berthon who was vicar of Romsey from 1860 to 1892; it was the first collapsible boat to be invented and the original, which is still in good con-

dition, is at Greenwich Maritime Museum. Many Berthon boats were made for recreational use, and they were popular on liners too. The Watcombe model was made about 1912; the cream slip boat is decorated with scrolls and running bands of 'commas' and is inscribed:

All good men must keep afloat
If they set sail in a Berthon boat.

The models were possibly made to stand on the counters of yacht chandlers, or they may have been a 'free gift' for the children of purchasers of a Berthon boat.

74

'Breweriana'

The Torquay Potteries also made a great variety of advertising pieces connected with the wines, spirits and brewing trades, and some of these are illustrated. The most common items were jugs, matchstrikers and ash-trays, suitable for use in pubs. Jugs were usually standard Torquay lines, such as an Aller Vale example decorated with a scandy pattern inviting customers to 'Drink Carnes well matured spirits'; this possibly refers to Messrs. W. & E. Carnes brewery at Falmouth which was bought out by Devenish in 1921. Heatherdale whisky jugs sometimes have a very distinctive asymmetrical scandy pattern which is believed to have been the work of one particular decorator about the time of World War I; similar

scandies are also seen on Quants violets bottles. Watcombe made at least two sizes of jugs advertising Rutherford and Kays Dreadnought whisky and these were decorated with a blue forget-me-not design. More unusual is the jug, also made by Watcombe, for Thorrocks Ales and Stout which is decorated with a tree, presumably intended to represent the Thor Oak; it is inscribed on the back 'Seabrooke and Sons Ltd. Established 1799. Grays, Essex'.

Matchstrikers were made to adver-tise 'Hall and Woodhouse' Brewery at Blandford, Dorset, Mappins Scotch Whiskey, or mineral water manufac-turers such as Biscombe's and Saluta-ris (fig. 62). The Salutaris Water Company, whose slogan was 'None so nice as Sally' also commissioned

Fig. 63. 'Breweriana'. Left to right: Matchstriker advertising John Groves and Sons of Weymouth (note incorrect spelling of Growes!) which is also a commemorative of the Coronation in 1902; Beer jug by Watcombe, inscribed on the reverse 'Seabrooke and Sons Ltd. Established 1799, Grays, Essex'; Dartmouth ashtray advertising 'St. Austell ales'; jug made by the Crown Dorset Pottery decorated with a thatched pub to advertise Whitbreads Ales; matchstriker advertising Hall and Woodhouse of Blandford. The John Groves and Hall and Woodhouse matchstrikers are both stamped on the base 'Sir J. Causton and Sons'.

75

Fig. 64. Items made to advertise spirits. Jugs, left to right: Pint and one and a half pint jugs advertising Dreadnought Scotch Whiskey – made by Watcombe and decorated with a forget-me-not pattern; 'Carnes' jug by Aller Vale; one and a half and one pint jugs made by Watcombe to advertise Heatherdale Scotch Whisky – note the asymmetrical scandy pattern on the jug on the right. Ashtrays advertising 'La Riva Sherry' and 'Grand Marnier' both by Watcombe; Mappins Brewery matchstriker and Golfers Liqueur Whiskey ashtray both with J.Causton mark and believed to be Watcombe.

CAMWAL

Like the BRITISH FLEET
FIRST IN ALL WATERS.

SODA WATER,
  POTASH WATER,
        LEMONADE,
GINGER ALE,
LIME JUICE and SODA,
ORANGE CHAMPAGNE, etc., etc.
in Syphons and Bottles.

—

DRY GINGER ALE.
TONIC WATER.

—

Old fashioned GINGER BEER in
Bottles and One Gallon Jars

advertising inkwells, perhaps for use by the publican when ordering their products!

One company that ordered extensively from the Watcombe Pottery was Camwal Ltd. of Starbeck, Harrogate, Yorkshire, who began producing soda and mineral waters c.1880. The company's full name was 'Chemists Aerated and Mineral Water Association Limited' which formed the acronym Camwal. By the 1920s their advertisement claimed 'Like the British fleet, first in all waters' – their range included lemonade, ginger beer, lime juice and orange champagne! Their advertising pottery includes large combination matchstrikers/ashtrays, small round coasters decorated with scandy patterns or a rural scene (presumably a local view) and black and yellow Art Deco style ashtrays. Camwal's went out of business about 1960.

Collectors should also look for a rare combination advertising commemorative made for Groves Brewery of Weymouth in 1902 (some of these are incorrectly inscribed Growes!). John Groves and Sons Ltd. were brewers, and wine and spirit merchants operating from Hope Square, Weymouth, Dorset. In 1902 the premises were reorganised and enlarged and this possibly prompted their decision to commission match-strikers which would commemorate this event and the Coronation. It was quite common for brewers to distribute gifts to the licencees of their tied houses and, if this is the case with these, then only about 120 would have been made. John Groves placed an advertisement in the Coronation Supplement to the Weymouth 'Telegram' of June 13th 1902 for their 'Mild and Pale ales, Nourishing and Extra Stout, for family use in small casks, from 4/6d. per Pin, and the same in bottles, from 2/6d. per dozen'. A pin was four and a half gallons, enough for any family to toast the new King's health! Groves later achieved a certain 'fame' as one of the first breweries in Britain to introduce beer in cans (just before World War II), anticipating the market for take-home sales. Even this was not enough to secure the future of the company because in 1960 they merged with Devenish, their neighbours in Hope Square.

Ashtrays also figure largely as alcohol advertising wares; often these are the standard rectangular shape inscribed with trade names such as 'La Riva Sherry' or 'Grand Marnier'. Collectors should also look for more unusual examples such as a horseshoe shaped tray with a shell pattern in relief in the centre which is inscribed 'Golfers Liqueur Whiskey' (fig. 64). This ashtray, like so many other examples of 'breweriana' does not carry a pottery backstamp but an impressed mark for 'Sir Joseph Causton & Sons Ltd. London'. This company was well known as printers, with their head office in Eastcheap, London. Their advertisements in commercial directories from 1900 list their business as printers, stationers, engravers, framers etc. with slight variations in the following years, none of which indicates their business in advertising wares! Yet, this was obviously a substantial sideline because, in addition to the Torquay Potteries, they also commissioned advertising wares from other potteries, such as those in Staffordshire; all those seen, have been connected with brewing.

Sometimes collectors may come across Torquay type jugs advertising Whitbreads Ales (fig. 63). These were made by the Crown Dorset Pottery at Poole and are attractively decorated with a thatched pub; they usually have a s'graffito motto:

'In Summer's heat,
In Winter's Gales,
Naught is so sweet as Whitbread's ales.'

Fig. 65. Detail to show impressed mark for Sir J. Causton and Sons Ltd., London. There are several variations of this mark, one being oval in shape.

A SOUVENIR FROM THE OLDEST
CHYMIST SHOPPE IN ENGLAND

Fig. 66. Selection of items all advertising The Oldest Chymist Shoppe at Knaresborough, Yorkshire. Most were made by Watcombe or Longpark, although the scent bottle was made by Royal Torquay and the egg cup decorated with a cottage by the Babbacombe Pottery. Many items have mottoes in Yorkshire dialect.

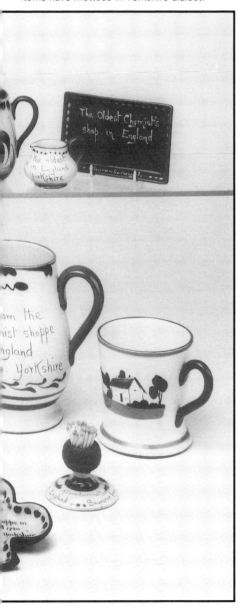

Collectors just beginning to specialise in Torquay advertising ware may become discouraged because some are so hard to find. If this is the case, why not start with pieces relating to the Oldest Chymist Shoppe at Knaresborough, Yorkshire, because there are plenty of these around (fig. 66).

The Oldest Chymist Shoppe is situated in the centre of Knaresborough at 16 The Market Place. It has been a pharmacy at least since 1720 although older herbals were found on the premises which suggest it may have been in business earlier. In the mid 1860s the shop came into the ownership of the Lawrence family, with father and son running it until 1965. It was during this time that souvenirs made by the Torquay Potteries were sold in the shop; most date from the 1920s and 1930s, although some were still being commissioned in the 1950s – the later pieces usually adopting the modern spelling 'Chemists Shop'!

Almost all sizes and styles of jugs and bowls seem to have been made, also beakers, ashtrays, cups and saucers, condiment sets, egg cups etc. Most of these are decorated with cream slip and a s'graffito inscription surrounded by simple slip dots and scrolls; sometimes scandies and cottages are also included, or, rarely, cockerels. More unusual are mugs and ashtrays with a piped inscription on a green slip ground, although their plainness makes them less attractive. Occasionally mottoes in Yorkshire dialect are added, such as 'Mak thisen at hooam' or 'Get hod of all tha can'. Collectors should also look for the rarer items such as inkwells, puzzle jugs and three horned vases.

The Oldest Chymist Shoppe was famous for its exclusive Lavender Water, which was exported all over the world. Many scent bottles were made for them by the Royal Torquay

Pottery, mostly decorated with a sprig of Lavender, although some had primroses instead and were filled with 'Eau de Cologne'.

The Shop retains much of its old world character and is filled with momentoes of the past (no Torquay pottery though). Modern visitors still like to go home with 'A souvenir of the Oldest Chymist Shoppe in England' although nowadays these are more likely to be tins of biscuits, jams or jars of sweets!

Yorkshire dialect mottoes on items from The Oldest Chymist Shoppe:

Get hod of all tha can
(Get hold of all you can).

Hear all, See all, Say Nowt
If tha doas oot for nowt
Allus do it for thisen.
(Hear all, See all, say nothing
If you do something for nothing
Always do it for yourself).

Help thisen to t'butter
(Help yourself to the butter).

Tak hod an sup
(Take hold and drink – on a cup).

Better be thrang ner dewin nowt
(Better be busy than doing nothing).

Mak thisen at hooam
(Make yourself at home).

Put t'wood in t'wa
(Put the wood in the wall i.e. Close the door!).

Shops

Numerous shops from all over Britain, and even abroad, chose to order their advertising wares from the Torquay Potteries – testimony, perhaps, to the advertising skills of the Potteries themselves! Many of these items were ashtrays, to be used in the shop, or to be given to well-esteemed customers, although jugs, mugs and plates have also been seen.

The blue ashtray made by Longpark for A. F. Roberts (fig. 67) must surely take the prize for being the most crammed, although for the local historian the information can be invaluable! A. F. Roberts ran a ladies and gents hairdressers at Reddenhill Road, Babbacombe during the 1930s; in addition to this, the ashtray states he also dealt in Tobacco, cigarettes, Pipes and Fancy goods! Mr. Roberts was a founder member of the Babbacombe and St. Marychurch Traders and Hoteliers Association; another founder member was Mr. Lowndes-Patemen whose perfumery (specialising in Devon violets!) filled many of the scent bottles made by the local Potteries.

By contrast, the round ashtray produced for Gristwoods Furnishing Stores, New Barnet, is very plain, containing simply the name of the

Fig. 67. Longpark ashtray for A. F. Roberts.

store done in s'graffito through a cream slip under an amber glaze (fig. 68). Mr. F. Gristwood first opened a drapers shop in East Barnet Road, New Barnet in 1896, but by the 1920s they had expanded to become a large department store offering 'every requirement for personal wear and for domestic use'. The store closed about 1970.

Many ashtrays simply advertise the name of the shop with no indication where they were. This can be very frustrating to the collector who wants to know more about the background to a new find – its always worth asking the dealer who sold the pot if they know anything about its origins, and local libraries often have old commercial directories to help in the search, but its a time consuming hobby! Investigations have identified Butler

Fig. 68. Selection of items to advertise shops. Left to right at the back: Longpark ashtray advertising Butler Morris Men's shop in Nottingham; vase with handle decorated with a yellow canary on a streaky black ground – made by Watcombe but stamped on the base: 'Jarrold Canary ware Regd. Norwich'. Jarrold's is a large department store in Norwich; Watcombe vase six and a half inches (16.5 cms.) tall decorated with a bright pink poppy, with a black painted inscription on the base 'Ranelagh C. R. & Co.' which is the name of an outlet; mug and plate made by Dartmouth and decorated with a view of The Little Chapel, Les Vauxbelets, Guernsey – stamped on the base 'Hand made in England by Dartmouth Pottery Ltd. for Williamson, Guernsey'. These pieces were decorated by Harry Crute and the mug is unusual in that his initials 'H.E.C.' appear to the right of the church. Middle row, left to right: Teastrainer bowl decorated with a cottage and made by the St.Marychurch Pottery for 'The Old Smithy' which is incised on the side of the pot and stamped on the base – a late advertising item made during the 1960's; two Watcombe jugs for 'G. J. Grose, Slades Supply Stores, St. Austell', dated Christmas 1956. Bottom row: Ashtray made by Longpark for Soyer and Son at Yeovil; ashtray to advertise Gristwood's Furnishing Stores at New Barnet – unmarked but probably Hart and Moist; Longpark ashtray inscribed 'A. E. Knight & Son, Ironmongers Tel: 82194'.

Gristwood's Furnishing Stores

Proprietor : F. J. Griſtwood.

34 & 36, EAST BARNET ROAD
NEW BARNET

YOUR HOME—

A single piece—a room full
or a housefull. We can supply
it, also every description of
kitchenware — glass — china,
etc. Bedding re-made same
day. Upholstery work.
Estimates given. . . . .

Morris on a square Longpark ashtray
decorated with a scandy pattern as
being a men's shop in Nottingham.
They began business c.1913 in Rad-
ford Road, and by 1956 they had expanded to four shops, all in
Nottingham – they closed in 1977. The
ashtray dates from the 1930s and has
the amusing inscription 'I aluz gits me
cloze frum Butler Morris'.

Two variations of ashtray have
been seen advertising Soyer and Son,
who owned a shop in Prince's Street,
Yeovil, from about the time of World
War 1 until the 1960s. The shop was
originally a fishmongers although later on they also sold meat; the Longpark ashtrays are either round or
novelty fish shaped pieces recalling
their early trade. Some pots still
remain mysteries though, such as a
St. Marychurch bowl with 'The Old

Smithy Pottery' on the base, a Longpark round ashtray for 'A. E. Knight
ironmongers' (possibly a Torquay
shop) and a Babbacombe ashtray decorated with a cottage and inscribed
'Conway Valley Nurseries for Trees
and Shrubs'; this dates from the
1950s.

Another late advertising piece is a
small cream jug which is inscribed
'With compliments G. J. Grose Slades
Supply Stores, St. Austell Christmas
1956'. This is one of the most common
shapes made by the Watcombe Pottery and was given the shape code
1476; the decoration is a cottage with
an inglenook – a style made popular
by Harry Crute. In the 1930s William
Howard Grose had a small general
store at 101 Slades Road, St. Austell;
at a later date the shop was taken over
by his son, 'G. J.' who moved to 105

Slades Road – the store is now believed to be owned by the Co-op.

Collectors should perhaps remember that sometimes the advertising element of a pot appears on the base and it is therefore worth examining all Torquay Pottery! Usually these are names of retailers, such as Middletons China Stores in Newton Abbot, who were a major outlet for the local potteries during the 1920's and 30's. Of the earlier examples, vases and jugs decorated with a yellow canary on a streaky black ground were made for Jarrolds Store in Norwich in the early 1900's and are often impressed 'Jarrold Canary Ware'. These were made by the Watcombe Pottery, as were vases decorated with a pink poppy on a cream ground inscribed 'Ranelagh CR & Co.' – so far the location of this outlet is unknown. Some Dartmouth mugs and plates have been seen which are stamped on the base 'Made by the Dartmouth Pottery Ltd. for Williamson Guernsey'; these are painted with a view of 'The Little Chapel, Les Vauxbelets, Guernsey' which was done by Harry Crute – collectors should look for examples which he signed with his initials 'HEC'.

Fig. 69. Devon Tors teapot made to advertise the Pear Tree Cafe which was at Ashburton, Devon.

ROYAL DEVONSHIRE CHINA.

VISITORS TO PLYMOUTH SHOULD SEE OUR STOCK OF THIS CELEBRATED "MOTTO" WARE. IMMENSE VARIETY HELD.

A NOVELTY.—TEAPOT, 2 CUPS and SAUCERS, SUGAR BASIN; and CREAM DISH (on Tray), extremely dainty, in the Royal China, in the correct shade of Green, 4s. 6d. complete.

IRONMONGERY SECTION.

CUTLERY,—REMARKABLE OFFER: SHEFFIELD. MADE TABLE KNIVES, with excellent Ivory Imitation Handles, guaranteed to keep colour, full table size, now offered 8s. 11d. per dozen. Cheese axe, 7s. 11d. per dozen. Ask to see this line; it is worthy inspection. THE "DAIRY" VACUUM CLEANER, no more dirt and dust, no more confusion, from £3 3s. each. Can be seen at work in our Showrooms every Afternoon from 2.30 to 4.30.

SPECIAL FÊTE GOWNS.

NEW WHITE MUSLIN BLOUSES, "Magyar" Style, Peter Pan Collars, at 3s. 11½d.
NEW CREAM SILK BLOUSES, "Magyar" Style, Peter Pan Collars, from 6s. 11½d.
NEW SILK BLOUSES, in Cream and other New Shades, "Magyar" Style, with the New Dutch Neck, from 21s. 9d
NEW LACE OVERSLIPS, in Ivory and Paris, New Designs, from 12s. 11d.
CHARMING NINON OVERSLIPS, in Navy, Grey, Royal, and Cream, from 29s. 9d.
NEW OSTRICH BOAS, in all Colours, from 12s. 11d.
SMART SICILIAN DUST WRAPS, Fawn, Grey, Navy, from 12s. 11d.
NEW SHANTUNG DUST COATS and WRAPS, from 29s. 6d.

Post Orders receive prompt attention. Our Post Order Staff buying over the counter obtain on your behalf every possible advantage.

SPOONER & CO., Ltd.,
PLYMOUTH and FALMOUTH.

83

ROYAL OAK HOTEL, KESWICK.

ANNUAL CARNIVAL BALL.
BOXING DAY.
FULLY BOOKED.

SPECIAL CINDERELLA DANCE.
SATURDAY, DECEMBER 23rd.

GALA DINNER AND DANCE,
NEW YEAR'S DAY,

Dinner, 7 p.m. Dancing from 8-30
p.m. to 2-30 a.m.

16/- per Couple or 8/6 Single.

Please ring up Keswick 23 and book
your tables in advance.

Hotels and nightclubs

It would be possible to build up a sizeable collection of ashtrays advertising hotels as there are so many of them! Most are for local hotels in the South Devon area and decorations range from the popular cottagewares as for Hylton Court Hotel, to the Art Deco mosaic pattern favoured by Andertons Hotel (fig. 70). More unusual, though, were those made by Watcombe for the Royal Oak Hotel at Keswick which were made as Christmas souvenirs. The hotel organised numerous events over Christmas and

Fig. 70. Selection of Watcombe ashtrays all advertising hotels.

Fig. 71. Selection of items advertising hotels and nightclubs. Top row, left to right: Watcombe ashtray decorated in Art Deco style inscribed 'Le bon viveur' – probably a nightclub; brown jug with blue cameo painted with yachts and a palm tree advertising 'The San Remo Hotel' – unmarked but probably Royal Torquay; Dartmouth mug and ashtray for 'Devon Coast Country Club'. Middle row, left to right: Watcombe bowl, Royal Torquay gypsy crock on three feet decorated with a Kingfisher on a blue ground; Royal Torquay bowl. Bottom row, left to right: Watcombe ashtray; Royal Torquay bowl; Watcombe ashtray. The triangular shaped ashtrays are decorated in bright colours and were for use in nightclubs.

the New Year including a Cinderella Dance on Christmas Eve, a Carnival Ball on Boxing Day and a Gala Dinner and Dance on New Year's Day – all were very popular and booked up well in advance. The rectangular ashtrays with small Art Deco motifs in the corners were presumably given to these customers because they are inscribed 'Health and Happiness to you and yours from the Royal Oak Hotel, Keswick' with the date – so far two variations have been seen, for 1936 and 1939, although possibly others will come to light.

Ashtrays made to advertise London nightclubs also favoured colourful Art Deco designs; the inscriptions were usually in French too, presumably to give them a slightly 'risque' image! However the more sober Devon Coast Country Club at Paignton chose the conventional cottage design for their ashtrays and mugs which were commissioned from the Dartmouth Pottery in the 1950s.

THE POTTERIES OWN
ADVERTISING PIECES

In addition to providing souvenir wares for sale all over Britain (and abroad) the Torquay Potteries were also tourist attractions in themselves. A Longpark advertisement in the Herald and Express of September 5th 1936 invited visitors to 'See the potters at work' and stressed that this was 'free'! A visit to one of the local potteries was on the itinerary of almost all the conferences and sporting tours held in South Devon; Mrs. Elsie Medland, who worked at Longpark from 1914 to 1957, recalled that 'often there were six or seven charas lined up in the drive!' In addition to seeing the potters at work, tourists were encouraged to visit the showroom where they could buy all the standard lines of pottery. It was also possible to order personal commemoratives or, in some cases, for visitors to inscribe their own pots, collecting them when they had been fired – generally about a week later. Devon Tors also allowed some visitors to paint their own designs on pots, especially plaques, and these are often signed on the back by the artist.

The Longpark Pottery seems to have been the only one to produce special souvenir wares depicting the pottery. Some of these were in the form of plates, decorated with a view of the pottery, or mugs and cups incised with a special motto (fig. 72).

This cup was made at Longpark
In Torquay by the sea
May health and happiness be
  theirs
Whoever drinks from thee.

For the Torquay pottery collector, the most highly prized advertising piece

---

VISITORS-FREE
SEE THE POTTERS AT WORK
Rain or Shine, Visitors will find
there is no greater interest than
a visit to the
LONGPARK POTTERIES
Newton Road — Torquay
Buses pass the entrance every
7 minutes and will stop by
request

HOURS OF INSPECTION 9.30 a.m.
to 5 p.m.

---

must be the shop signs advertising the pottery. These are quite rare, even though many hundreds must have been made for the shops that sold the pottery. The Watcombe display stands are three and a half inches tall and are moulded in relief in the form of a cottage; the inglenook fireplace and quality of decoration suggest they were done by Harry Crute. Longpark made a similar cottageware version. The Dartmouth stands are eight and a half inches tall, and are moulded in the shape of a galleon; these are dark brown, the colour of early Dartmouth pottery from the 1950s. By contrast the St. Marychurch Pottery advertising stands are small shells, decorated with a cottage and the name of the Pottery.

The most splendid advertising piece of them all must be the plate made for Spooners advertising the Royal Aller Vale and Watcombe Potteries (Outside Back Cover). It is decorated with blue irises, done in faience style on a cream ground. This decoration was first used in the early 1900s and continued to be popular for about

Fig. 72. Items made to advertise the potteries. Left to right: giant cup and saucer decorated with the scandy pattern and motto which begins 'This cup was made at Longpark'; round plate with a pigment painted view of the Longpark Pottery; shop stand decorated with a cottage advertising 'Royal Watcombe Pottery'; dark brown and amber ship advertising Dartmouth Pottery; small shell shaped stand inscribed 'Traditional Devon Pottery made by The St.Marychurch Pottery Ltd., Torquay Devon'. Dartmouth stand eight and a half inches (21.5 cms.) tall.

20 years. Spooners was a large department store in Plymouth and they sold a wide variety of Torquay pottery. In March 1911 they held a special Crafts Week and one of the attractions was 'the potter modelling at his wheel' – it is very likely this potter came from the Aller Vale or Watcombe Potteries as many employees were sent on similar publicity campaigns to large stores. A Spooners advertisement in the Illustrated Western Weekly News of June 3rd 1911 stated: 'Royal Devonshire China. Visitors to Plymouth should see our stock of this celebrated 'Motto' Ware. Immense variety held. A novelty – teapot, two cups and saucers, sugar basin and cream dish (on Tray), extremely dainty . . . in the correct shade of green, 4s. 6d. complete' (22p.). Spooners store was bombed out during the blitz on Plymouth in March 1941 – fortunately the plate survived.

Fig. 73. Elsie Franks and Charlie Skinner in the slip-dipping shop at the Longpark Pottery in 1920.

MAKING COMMEMORATIVES

Cyril Wilson worked at the Watcombe and Longpark Potteries after World War II following in his father, Reginald Wilson's footsteps; he is therefore familar with the techniques and processes of making commemoratives, especially as his father had been responsible for the 1953 and 1937 Watcombe models. Mr. Wilson has estimated the labour required to produce 300 commemorative beakers of the type produced for Cookham Dean in 1902 as:

Wedging and weighing clay	3 hours
Throwing	8 hours
Turning	8 hours
Dipping (outside)	3 hours
Dipping (inside)	2$\frac{1}{2}$ hours
Sprigging	12 hours
Decorating	8 hours
Inscribing	6 hours
Glazing	2 hours
Kiln Placing	1$\frac{1}{2}$ hours
TOTAL	54 hours

These estimates do not allow for breakages and, obviously, the overall production time would be longer because of drying and firing times at various stages. The Cookham Dean beakers, including carriage, cost £9.15.1d.(£9.75), a low sum even in those days for fiftyfour hours of labour, some of which involved considerable skill.

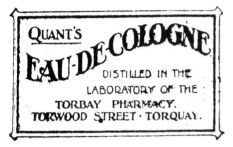

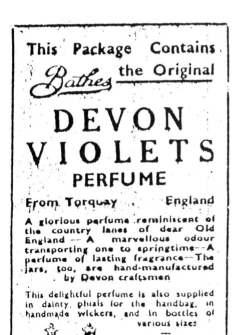

Sweet smell of success

Scent bottles formed a major part of the output of the Torquay Potteries and many were made to advertise chemists shops, and other retailers; these have the added advantage of taking up very little space and still being modestly priced (fig. 74).

The earliest scent bottles were made in the 1890s by the Watcombe Pottery and usually formed part of dressing table sets. By the early 1900s other potteries began to make them too, especially Longpark, and they were decorated with the popular mottoware designs of scandies, cockerels and ships together with a suitable motto. Soon, some of these were inscribed with the name of the chemist shop, such as 'Quants', a pharmacy in Torwood Street, Torquay, which distilled its own 'Eau de Cologne'. Although there is no pottery stamp, the thickly incised s'graffito lettering is typical of the Longpark Pottery. The pot is decorated with an asymmetrical scandy pattern which appeared on a variety of items made during the first decade or so of this century.

Just after World War I a new scent bottle was introduced, decorated with a mauve violet on a cream ground, which became an instant success with tourists. The Longpark Pottery claimed to be the originator of the design, although there is no firm evidence of this, and soon virtually all the Torquay Potteries were producing similar versions – they were still being made by the Dartmouth Pottery in the late 1950s. Although violets was the most popular perfume, many others were produced too, such as lavender, rose, lily of the valley, lilac, mixed bouquets and even sea breezes! Many of these scent bottles are inscribed with the name of the retailer, usually as part of the inscription although sometimes on the base. Local shops

89

are, quite naturally, the most common, but other outlets are found from all over Britain and even Ireland.

Small 'squashy' shaped violet bottles are the most common; these were made simply by shaping the ball of clay in the hand and pushing a finger in to make the scent container. Retailers names found on some of these include Vickery Bros. and Dell-ers, both of Paignton, Windles of Swanage and Stirlings True Irish Violets. Another common shape was the sloping sided churn favoured by Devon Tors and Longpark – these were made to hold 'Bristow's Old Devon Violets' scent and Old English Lavender from Evans Chemists at Margate, amongst others.

More unusual shaped scent bottles include an elegant jug with handle

Fig. 74. Selection of advertising scent bottles.

made to hold 'Bathes Devon Violet bath cologne'. Bathes drug stores were in Fleet Street, Torquay, and they had their own laboratory for filling the pots with scent. In the 1930s Bathes sold four sizes of perfume: 1 oz. size sold for 1/6d. (seven and a halfpence), 2 oz. sold for 2/6d. (twelve and a halfpence), 4 oz. sold for 4/6d. (twenty two and a halfpence), and the 6 oz. sold for 7/6d. (thirty seven and a halfpence). In 1934 Bathes mounted an exhibition of Devon Violet perfume at the South London Exhibition, Crystal Palace, London; the Torquay Times informed its readers that the stand 'is in violet and silver, while rustic wood taken from Bovey Tracey, has gone to the making of it'. Although Bathes were famous for their violet perfume they also made other scents such as lily of the valley.

Boots the Chemists ordered a wide variety of scent bottles from several Torquay Potteries and these could form a small collection in themselves. Violets bottles were usually made by the Longpark Pottery and came in several shapes; collectors should look for the more unusual bulbous pots with long thin necks. The Pottery attempted to copy the Boots logo in the inscription but it is not always successful. During the 1930s Boots ordered colourful Art Deco style scent pots which included crudely sponged 'blobs' of pigment outlined in black from the Royal Torquay Pottery, a band of mosaic colours on a blue pot from Watcombe and bunches of hanging fruit on a black and tan pot from the Daison Art Pottery; in all cases the Boots logo appears as a black stamp on the base. Most scent bottles seem to have lost their stoppers or else contain a plain metal capped cork. However collectors should look for crown stoppers and the rare pixies and imps, and for bottles which still have their original plastic film and ribbons. Sometimes bottles can be found which contain glass phials of scent, such as the one for Corrie's of Grasmere – this was a cheaper method of filling the bottles than the laborious task of individual filling using a pipette. It is also worth looking at the unusual shaped pots such as a lighthouse or a mushroom – so far none have been seen that are advertising pieces, but there may be some that will turn up!

Advertising scent bottles

Corrie's Grasmere Violets (Devon Tors).

Carters of Penzance.

Steven's Chemist – Hove (Devon Tors).

Devon Violets.
Vickery Bros. Paignton (?Watcombe).

English Lakes bouquet.
Norman Hodgson Chemist Keswick (Devon Tors).

Ilfracombe breezes.
Reeds Chemist – Ilfracombe. (Longpark and Watcombe).

Oldest Chymist Shoppe, Knaresborough. (Royal Torquay).

Quants Eau de Cologne.
Distilled in Torquay (Longpark).

Stirlings True Irish violets. (Devon Tors).

Old English Lavender.
Evans Chemist Margate (Longpark).

Dorset Violets.
Windles Chemist Swanage (Watcombe).

Boots the Chemists (various potteries).

Bathes Devon Lily.
Torquay England (?Watcombe).

Bathes Devon Violets Bath Cologne.
Torquay England.
Heaven send thee many merry days (?Watcombe).

the Original

DEVON VIOLETS

PERFUME

From Torquay England

Devon Violets.
Dellers Pharmacists Paignton (Watcombe).

Ye Olde Devon Violets.
Bristow's. (Devon Tors).

'Lyonesse'
Peasgood Penzance. (Longpark).
(Lyonesse was the lost Kingdom where King Arthur's Knights rode – it was off the coast of Cornwall).

Gregorys Dorset Violets (Devon Tors).

Colsons Sale Notice in the Express and Echo, June 24 1933, relating to the Exeter Cathedral Anniversary Commemorative mentioned on page 44.

Take home to your friends a souvenir from

COLSONS
OF EXETER
The Shopping Place of the County

. SALE .

NOTICE

In deference to the expressed wish of our Civic Authorities, that during the Cathedral Festival Week our shops shall be looking their very best, we have altered the opening date of our Summer Sale to Monday, July 3rd, as we feel that shop windows are not at their best when filled with Sale goods.

We believe Ladies generally will appreciate our action and will be content to postpone their Sale purchases until this later date.

Next week, however, we shall offer New Season's Goods at such remarkable prices, as will effectively demonstrate to the thousands of visitors, the advantages of Exeter – and Colsons in particular – as a shopping centre.

COLSONS OF EXETER
The Shopping Place of the County

Advertising mottoes

Drink Carnes well matured spirits.

Drink Ye Olde 'Heatherdale' Malt
  Whiskey
Ye finest made in Scotland.

Drink DREADNOUGHT Scotch
  Whisky
The best of all.

In Summers Heat
In Winters Gales
Nought is so sweet
As WHITBREADS ALES.

Try Hunts Pure Cider
On draught and in bottle.

Here Meda Cider is made
Meadhay, Dunsford, Devon.

Henley's Cyder
Cock of the Walk
(on a Longpark jug decorated with a
  black cockerel).

Come fill me full with liqour (sic)
  sweet
For that is good when friends do
  meet
But pray take care don't let me fall
Lest you lose your liqour jug and all.
(On a Henley's Cider jug).

All good men must keep afloat
If they set sail in a Berthon boat.

J. W. Humphrey's and Son
A small piece of Devonshire Ware
Wishing our friends a Happy New
  Year.

Best wishes from Soyer and Son
A pla(i)ce for ashes
(On Longpark fish shaped ashtray).

I aluz gits me cloze from Butler
  Morris.

L. O. R. Tweddle and Co. Ltd.
  Capsule Makers
297 Goswell Rd., London E.C.1.
'Pessimism never paid a dividend'

A present from Hylton Court Hotel,
  Torquay.

Health and happiness to You and
  Yours
From the Royal Oak Hotel Keswick
Xmas 1939.

Xmas 1928
Ye Olde Dick Turpin Lodge
Chudleigh R.A.O.B.
(Devon Tors mug).

—
CAMWAL, LIMITED,
Starbeck, Harrogate,
And at London, Manchester. Birmingham,
and Bristol.

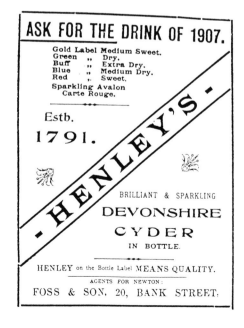

ASK FOR THE DRINK OF 1907.

Gold Label Medium Sweet.
Green   „   Dry.
Buff   „   Extra Dry.
Blue   „   Medium Dry.
Red   „   Sweet.
Sparkling Avalon
  Carte Rouge.

Estb.
1791.

HENLEY'S

BRILLIANT & SPARKLING

DEVONSHIRE
CYDER
IN BOTTLE.

HENLEY on the Bottle Label MEANS QUALITY.

AGENTS FOR NEWTON :

FOSS & SON, 20, BANK STREET.

BOTTLED SUNSHINE AND OTHER COALS
LOWEST SUMMER PRICES.

T. B. PURNELL & SONS, 263, HIGH-ST., EXETER.
Agents for the " UNION-CASTLE " Mail Steamship Co., Ltd.

Companies shops, brand names etc. which were advertised on Torquay pottery

Andertons Hotel (Watcombe).

Barton Hall, Torquay (Watcombe).
Berthon Boat Company, Romsey (Watcombe).
Biscombes Mineral Waters (Causton/Watcombe)
Blue Ball Inn, Lynmouth (Watcombe).
A. S. Burbank, Plymouth, Mass. U.S.A. (Aller Vale).
Butler Morris, Nottingham (Longpark).

Camwal (Chemists Aerated and Mineral Water Association Ltd.) Harrogate (Watcombe).
Canary Ware (Jarrolds of Norwich), (Watcombe).
Carnes Spirits (Aller Vale).
Conway Court Hotel (marked on base with the name of an outlet 'L. E. Fisher Ltd., Torquay'. Probably made by Royal Torquay).
Conway Valley Nurseries (Babbacombe).

Devon Coast Country Club (Dartmouth).
Dreadnought Whiskey (Rutherford and Kays), (Watcombe).
Dymchurch Holiday Camp (Royal Torquay).

Elfordleigh (Royal Torquay).

Golfers Liqueur Whisky (Causton/Watcombe).
Grand Marnier (Watcombe).
Gristwoods Furnishing Stores, New Barnet (?Hart and Moist).
G. J. Grose, Slades Supply Stores, St. Austell (Watcombe).
Groves Brewery, Weymouth (Causton/Watcombe).

Hall and Woodhouse, Blandford Forum (Causton/Watcombe).
Heatherdale Whisky (Watcombe).
Henley's Cyder (Longpark).
Hope and Anchor Inn (unmarked).
J. W. Humphrey's & Sons, Chadwell Heath (Longpark).
Hunts Cider (Longpark).
Hylton Court Hotel (Watcombe).

SYMONS'
GOLD MEDAL DEVONSHIRE CYDER

Head Office & Fruit Mills : TOTNES, DEVON. Phone: 8

LONDON (Office & Stores):—BUTCHER ROW, RATCLIFF, E. Phone: 3545 East

95

Jarrolds (Canary Ware) Norwich (Watcombe).
Journey's End Inn, Ringmore (probably Royal Torquay).

A. E. Knight Ironmonger (Longpark).

La Riva Sherry (Watcombe).
Le Bon Viveur (Watcombe).

Mappins Scotch Whisky.
Meadhay Ltd. (Cider). (Devon Tors).
Meadhurst, Torquay. (Watcombe).
Medina Court Hotel (Watcombe).
Middletons China Stores, Newton Abbot (various).

Old Commercial Inn, Bishopsteignton (Devon Tors).
Oldest Chymist Shoppe, Knaresborough (various).
Old Smithy Pottery (?St. Marychurch).

Palace Hotel Torquay (Watcombe).
A. F. Pears & Co. (Pears Soap), (Watcombe).
Pear Tree Cafe Ashburton (Devon Tors).
Priory Farm Dairy, Taunton (Watcombe).
T. B. Purnell & Co., Exeter (Purnells Bottled Sunshine), (Exeter Art Pottery).

Ranelagh C. R. & Co. (Watcombe).
A. F. Roberts, Babbacombe (Longpark).
Roslin Hall Hotel, Torquay (Watcombe).
Royal Oak Hotel, Keswick (Watcombe).
R.S.P.C.A. Fund for Sick and Wounded Horses (Watcombe).
Rutherford and Kay's Dreadnought Whisky (Watcombe).

Salutaris Water Co. (Watcombe).
San Remo Hotel (?Royal Torquay).
St. Marychurch and Babbacombe Y.M.C.A. (Longpark).

UNSOLICITED TESTIMONIALS
ARE CONTINUALLY BEING RECEIVED FOR THE EXCELLENCE OF OUR

BOTTLED SUNSHINE
(THE BEST COAL IN THE KINGDOM).

T. B. PURNELL & SONS,
EXETER.
TELEPHONE No. 39.

PALACE HOTEL
TORQUAY

Dine & Dance
in atmosphere
to

Jean Salder
and his broadcasting orchestra
•
DANCE with Clemson and Valerie
our Dance Host and Hostess